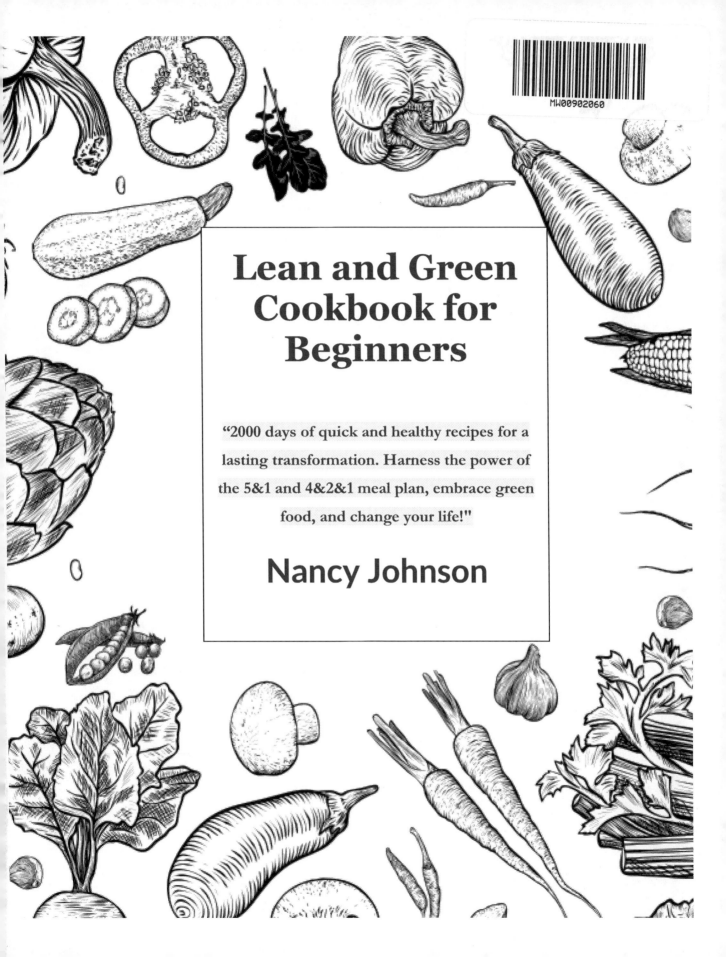

Lean and Green Cookbook for Beginners

"2000 days of quick and healthy recipes for a lasting transformation. Harness the power of the 5&1 and 4&2&1 meal plan, embrace green food, and change your life!"

Nancy Johnson

HEALTHY AND TASTY WITH
Nancy

Nancy

My mother loves cooking very much. When I was young, I was convinced that my name was 'Taste it'.
(Anonymous)

'Have you eaten?' Is the most authentic expression of love.
(Laura Morante)

One cannot think well, love well, sleep well, if one has not dined well.
(Virginia Woolf)

Nancy

Nancy

Dear Reader, welcome to the world of Health & Tasty with Nancy! I hope you will experience a delicious culinary journey through these pages. Creating this book has been a thrilling experience and I am so happy to share it with you.

But that's not all! I am very grateful that you chose my book and gave me the chance to share my passion with you. I would also like it if you could take one extra step and leave a review once you have finished reading. I would greatly appreciate your opinion and it would be wonderful if you could give me feedback on my book. This will allow me to continuously work on creating even richer and tastier content for you and for other readers like you.

I am truly grateful for this opportunity, for your choice, and for your trust. I can't wait to read your review and to have you join me on this fantastic journey! Happy reading!

Your Sincerly
Nancy

Table of Contents

Chapter no. 1 Introduction to Lean and Green Diet

In this chapter, you will learn about the basis of a lean and green diet and what is Optavia diet. The work of this diet to lose weight and the benefits and disadvantages of a lean and green diet are also discussed. A list of items you can use and the item you are not permitted to use is also given. Some tips you can use to succeed in this diet are also described in detail in this chapter.

Lean and Green Diet

Lean & Green meals are heavy in protein & low in carbohydrates. 5–7 ounces of prepared lean protein, 3 servings of non-starchy veggies, and up to two meals of healthy fats are included in each meal. The strategy also contains one optional snack daily, which the coach must allow. Similar to green diet, the lean & green diet substitutes lean protein sources for high-fat ones. Lean sources of protein often come from skinless chicken, fish (as cod & haddock), eggs, lean meat cuts, and plant proteins like lentils and beans. The research has yet to support the idea that lean diet is superior than a typical low-fat diet for anyone when it regards weight loss and health improvement. Recent research demonstrates that lean diets are as effective in reducing body mass as low fat diets. Additionally, compared to low-fat diets, these do not exhibit a noticeably better reduction in risk factors for disease such blood pressure, blood lipids, as well as insulin resistance. The lean & green diet seems to be a unique variation on the low-fat diet that uses lean proteins in place of fat to encourage weight reduction and reduce health risks. This sort of diet enhances metabolism by boosting metabolic rate, which expedites weight reduction. Because a lean & green diet doesn't really result in a significant rise in body fat compared to low-fat diets, it also lowers the risk of overweight. The focus is on additional protein-rich foods like eggs, beans and lentils in your diet along with modest portions of twice-daily meat and fish. In addition to vitamin-rich fruits, the diet also contains vegetables (e.g. carrots). Various kinds of beans, such as black-eyed peas, green lentils, & soybeans, are included in the category of green food. One of the balanced eating that ought to be regularly followed is Green and Lean diet since it balances out all other nutritious foods.

Versions of Diet

Two weight reduction plans, as well as a weight maintenance program, are included in lean and green or Optavia diet:

- 5&1 Plan: This diet, which is most often used, consists of 5 Optavia Fuelings & one healthy Lean & Green meal per day.
- 4&2&1: This menu comprises 4 Optavia Fuelings, 2 Lean & Green meals, & one snack each day for people who want extra calories or versatility in their eating options.
- The 3&3 Plan for Optimal Health: This maintenance-focused diet plan comprised of 3 Optavia Fuelings & three well-balanced Lean & Green meals daily.

Working of Lean and Green Diet

A marketed diet called lean and green diet necessitates the buying of pre-packaged foods called Fuelings, which can include soups, cereals, pasta, shakes, crunchy snacks, and bars. Fuelings are created for losing weight by doctors, nutritionists, and scientists. There are more than 50 alternatives, all of which, according to the manufacturer, are nutrient-dense & portion-controlled to promote digestive health, high-quality and complete protein, and 24 minerals and vitamins. As per Optavia, fuelings are created without artificial colors, flavors, or sweeteners. As a result, the daily caloric intake may range from 800-1,000 calories. Five of the six meals on the

famous Optimal Diet 5 & 1 Plan, which calls for small portions to be consumed every 2 to 3 hours Optavia Fuelings. You will be taught how to make your own Lean & Green meal for the 6th meal, which should include 5-7 ounces lean protein, 3 servings non-starchy veggies, and a maximum of two portions of good fats to maintain blood sugar levels. While on the diet, Optavia advises staying away from alcohol, sweetened beverages, solid shortening, plus high-calorie sweets. Optavia diet also includes a few items that are restricted initially but eventually reintroduced, including starchy vegetables (including maize, peas & potatoes), whole grain goods and low-fat dairy products.

Advantages and Disadvantages of Lean and Green Diet

Advantages

The major health advantage of implementing a Lean and Green diet is fast weight reduction, which is especially beneficial for persons who need to drop a lot of weight quickly.

1. Convenience

It's simple & handy to buy packaged, pre-portioned meals; there's no need to analyze calories or carbohydrates. It's also useful to have basic recipe for making the meals in home. In place of analyzing calories, you'll record servings of particular items, creating it simpler for tracking your meals.

2. Reduced obesity and overweight risks

Losing weight quickly provides two health advantages: People are more likely to lose weight & keep it off if they exercise regularly. If you're a huge amount of weight to drop, losing it quickly may improve your outcomes while also increasing your chances of long-term success. Obesity or being overweight might put you at risk for a variety of ailments. Hypertension, heart disease, type 2 diabetes, osteoarthritis, and many forms of cancer are only a few of them. Losing merely 5% of one's body weight may assist in mitigating these dangers.

3. Improved cholesterol and blood sugar levels

Although some health professionals advocate a 1-2 pounds of weight reduction each week, there are situations when a quicker pace is recommended. Rapid weight reduction, for example, has been linked to improved lipid & glycemic profiles. This suggests that persons who have high cholesterol & blood sugar concerns may benefit from reducing weight more quickly. However, slower rates of weight reduction resulted in better body makeup alterations.

4. Coaching support

Lean and Green also aid via its coaching session, which several users might find helpful. Coaching might help you in keeping on track and boosting the odds of success.

Disadvantages

There are several possible drawbacks to Lean and Green strategy that might have a negative impact on your health.

1. Nutrient deficiency

If calorie counts are maintained too low like that for so long, the diet might result in deficiencies of nutrition. In contrast to calorie limit, Lean and Green programs eliminate some food categories, such as fruits, vegetables, & whole grains, that all include critical minerals and vitamins.

2. Reduced sports routine

Rapid weight loss might have a negative impact on athletic performance. According to a survey of ten papers, although athletes wish to lose weight, achieving so too quickly might damage their ability while also putting their

health in danger. An extremely low-calorie diet is unlikely to sustain an athlete's intensive training schedule. If an athlete wishes to shed weight, several health professionals recommend doing it during the off-season, while training requirements are lower.

3. Sales pressure

Coaching assistance may sometimes be viewed as a disadvantage. Because of multi-level structure, many have dubbed the concept a pyramid scam. Users who finish the Lean and Green program are motivated to become trainers, market the company's goods, & recruit new salespeople. Potential clients may be put off by this.

4. Cost

This plan may be expensive; 5 fuelings would cost back about $17 before tax & delivery or the foodstuff you purchase for lean & green food.

5. Hunger

This method of weight loss is inconvenient but might not be long-term. Extreme hunger, exhaustion, and other unfriendly signs are mutual side effects of low-calorie diet. When you're hungry, it's easy to be induced to eat something that is not on the diet plan.

Things You Can Eat

You'll prepare 1-3 low-calorie food items for yourself, focusing on lean meat & non-starchy veggies.

1. Lean Protein

You have to include a 5-7-ounce serving of cooked lean meat in your lean & green meals. Using the examples provided, Lean and Green differentiate between leaner, lean, & leanest protein origins:

- Leaner: Chicken breast or swordfish
- Lean: Salmon, pork chops, or lamb
- Leanest: Cod, egg whites and shrimp

2. Non-Starchy Veggies

The 5&1 program from Lean and Green allows you to eat 2 veggies that are not starchy in addition to the proteins in your meal and these vegetables are grouped into 3 categories: low, intermediate, & high carbohydrates, with the examples given:

- Lower carb: Green Salad
- Intermediate carb: Summer squash or cauliflower
- Higher carb: Peppers or broccoli

3. Healthy Fats

Lean & green lunch may include up to 2 servings of good fats in combination to lean meat & non-starchy veggies.

- Avocado
- Walnut oil
- Olive oil
- Flaxseed

4. Low-Calorie Condiments

Certain condiments are allowed in your cooked dishes as part of a diet.

- Vinegar
- Mustard
- Herbs
- Lime
- Spices
- Lemon

- Salsa

5. Low-Fat Dairy, Fresh Fruit, and Whole Grains

The Lean and Green Diet enables you to increase your dairy, fruit, and grain intake after you've reached your optimum weight:

- Whole-grain bread, high-fiber cereals, whole wheat muffins, etc.
- Greek yogurt
- Cottage cheese
- Apples, berries, bananas, etc.

Things You Cannot Eat

Although no foods are legally limited on the Lean and Green diet, several are highly discouraged.

1. Desserts

The Lean & Green diet discourages consuming sweets to satisfy sugar cravings. After the initial weight loss phase, you may resume eating low-calorie sweet treats like fruit or yoghurt. However, you should stay away from the following:

- Ice cream
- Cookies
- Cakes

High-Calorie Additions

- Butter
- BBQ sauce that is sugary
- Mayonnaise

Sugar-Sweetened & Alcoholic Beverages

- Wine
- Sweet coffee beverages
- Soda
- Spirits
- Beer

Key points to Follow to be Successful with the Lean & Green Diet

1. Exercise Will Help

You were expecting that, and certainly, the recommendation to sometimes walk on a machine is always valid. Because nothing complements a diet better than a regular workout schedule, this doesn't, however, require you to join the nearby gym on a regular basis. You don't have to exhaust yourself, either. You can work out close to home if the thought of exercising in front of others makes you uncomfortable. Additionally, there are no regulations requiring you to engage in an intense workout that causes your guts to turn. The truth is that there are plenty of alternatives available to you when deciding which workout is best for you. In order to give you an idea, here are a few exercises that are quite popular yet do not need joining a gym.

- Pilates
- Yoga
- Swimming
- Dancing
- Cycling
- Running
- Walking
- Rowing

Most of these activities genuinely seem to be a lot of fun, as you'll see. However, the key is to select a workout that you like. Then plan your day in order to develop the habit. Therefore, consider which exercise will be simple to maintain over the long run rather than asking which workout would aid burn most calories.

2. Support System for Staying Motivated

Nobody can ever always be joyful and motivated. Cycle of various emotions is inherent to human existence. There can be times when you lack the motivation to follow the exercise or diet plan. These times are unavoidable, but they may also be risky. Because missing one day might easily result in giving oneself a pass for the remainder of the week. You wish to be ready for when one of those bad days comes. And developing a support network is among the finest methods to becoming ready. At end of day, having someone around to keep you encouraged is quite helpful, particularly on days that you doubt your ability to follow the plan.

3. Get Sufficient Sleep
Sleep is often taken for granted. As well as what they overlook is the profound effect that sleep can have on each and every individual. For instance, did you know that as you sleep, the body heals and grows muscular tissue? How about resetting the brain so that it will be alert the next day? How well one sleeps will have an impact on everything, from how you feel when you wake up to how the majority of the day goes. Now, when you consider how to lose that weight quicker on lean and green diet, the same principle still holds true. You restore a crucial balance when you allow your body ample time to relax and regenerate. You are also more secure in the new health decisions when you awake. Furthermore, you will be inspired to continue the excellent job you have been doing.

4. Be Proactive
Even the biggest victories in life began as baby steps. Additionally, despite the fact that the digital era has increased people's expectations for quick outcomes, tiny actions may ultimately result in significant improvements. In this situation, concentrate on being active at periods when you ordinarily sit or stand motionless. For instance, why don't you try to stand for a portion of the time if your job involves a lot of sitting? Additionally, why not take a stroll while on the phone? Every hour while watching television, stand up and jog for a few minutes in one spot. Park farther away from shop or place of employment and use the stairs rather than the elevator. Combining all the tiny things you do to be active and persevere will ultimately pay off. Keep in mind that your body rarely actually stops working, so everything you do has a permanent effect on it. Additionally, being active is not impossible simply because you aren't on football field or gym.

5. Program the Inner Voice
The most effective tool you have for making significant life changes is the inner voice. In fact, this might be the root cause of your weight issues in the initial place. Therefore, if you spend time evaluating your self-talk, would you say that it is encouraging or demeaning? It is essential to train the inner voice to act as an empowering force in the life if you wish to succeed on your weight reduction journey. But if you beat yourself up for every small thing, you will inevitably fail and end up feeling much worse. Realize that you're your own biggest adversary right now, and keep that in mind whenever you feel like giving up. Nobody else has the right to instruct you on how or what to feel. This freedom is unique to you.

6. A Mindful Lifestyle
As was previously said, following a diet alone won't help you lose weight. The pace and amount of weight loss will be influenced by other aspects and considerations. But why not use this chance to learn to make better decisions? Think about how your body responds to the foods and beverages you consume, for instance. And do you engage in any harmful behaviors, such as smoking? If you're serious about using lean and green diet to lose weight more quickly, examine your regular eating habits carefully.

In addition, this cookbook contains enough variety and number of recipes to cover a period of 2000 days.

Chapter no. 2 Breakfast Recipes

1. Chipotle Mac and Cheese Waffles

Prep time: 2mins

Cook time: 8mins

Servings: 2

Lean: 0

Green: 0

Condiments: 2-3

Ingredients
- 4 oz of egg substitute liquid
- 2 sachets of chipotle mac & cheese Optavia select
- 2 tablespoons of maple syrup sugar-free
- 1 teaspoon of hot sauce
- 1 can of cooking spray

Instructions
- Mix the water & chipotle mac and cheese well inside a bowl. 1 1/2 mins on high, then stir, for one minute of standing time, then stir and then let rest until chilled.
- Egg white fluid is whisked in.

- On a hot and oiled waffle iron, add the ingredients.
- Bake for 3-5 mins with the lid closed to ensure complete cooking.
- Take waffles out from waffle maker with caution, and if preferred, serve with maple syrup.

Nutrients: Calories: 751kcal, Carbs: 33g, Protein: 18g, Fat: 62g

2. Greek Yogurt Breakfast Bark

Prep time: 10mins

Cook time: 0mins

Servings: 2

Lean: 0

Green: 0

Condiments: 2

Ingredients
- 1 sachet of red berry crunchy o's cereal Optavia essential
- 1-2 packets of sugar substitute zero-calorie
- 12 oz of plain Greek yogurt non-Fat

Instructions
- Mix Greek yogurt & sugar substitute inside a bowl.
- Non-stick foil should be used to line baking dish. Greek yogurt should be evenly layered on baking dish's bottom.
- On top of yogurt, top with red berry Crunchy O's cereal.
- Until the bark is firm, chill for 4-5 hours.

- Use sharp knife to cut the bark into tiny chunks. Keep leftovers inside the freezer in containers.

Nutrients: Calories: 127kcal, Carbs: 18g, Protein: 11g, Fat: 5g

3. Avocado Toast

Prep time: 5mins

Cook time: 15mins

Servings: 1

Lean: 0

Green: 0

Condiments: 1

Ingredients

- 1 ½ oz of mashed Avocado
- 1 sachet of cheddar herb buttermilk biscuit Optavia select

Instructions

- Cook cheddar herb biscuit as directed on the packet. Bake inside a lightly oiled ramekin for optimal results.
- Add mashed Avocado on top after letting it cool.

Nutrients: Calories: 195kcal, Carbs: 20g, Protein: 5g, Fat: 11g

4. Honey Cinnamon Baked Oatmeal

Prep time: 5mins

Cook time: 25mins

Servings: 4

Lean: 0

Green: 0

Condiments: 3

Ingredients

- 4 sachets of honey and cinnamon hot cereal Optavia Indonesian
- 1/2 teaspoon of baking powder
- 1 cup of almond milk unsweetened
- 3 tablespoons of egg substitute liquid
- 1/4 tsp of cinnamon
- 1 can of cooking spray
- 11/3 oz of pecans
- 11/3 oz of walnuts

Instructions

- Set the oven at 350°F.
- Baking soda & Indonesian hot cereal with cinnamon & honey are combined in a big bowl.
- Stir till milk is completely absorbed after adding egg white & almond milk. Mix in the nuts.
- Four lightly oiled Mason jars should receive an equal amount of the mixture; leave approximately a half inch on the top.
- Sprinkle cinnamon over the tops.
- On a baking sheet, cook for 20-25 minutes, or till the top is somewhat hard and brown.
- Allow it to cool totally. Put on the lid, store in the fridge, and use before five days.

Nutrients: Calories: 214kcal, Carbs: 39g, Protein: 5g, Fat: 5g

5. Dash Mini Waffle Maker Omelet

Prep time: 5mins

Cook time: 5mins

Servings: 1

Lean: 0

Green: 0

Condiments: 2

Ingredients

- 2 tablespoons of finely chopped red bell peppers
- 6 tablespoons of egg substitute liquid
- 2 tablespoons of finely chopped onion
- 1 teaspoon of finely chopped jalapeno peppers
- 2 dash cooking spray
- 1 tablespoon of finely chopped raw spinach
- 1 tablespoon of salsa
- 1/4 cubed avocado

Instructions

- In a bowl, add spinach, egg whites, onion, bell pepper, and jalapeno, then mix vigorously.
- Spray top & bottom of the waffle maker using a non-stick spray, then pour in half the mixture.
- Close waffle maker, then let it bake for 3 to 4 minutes.
- Carefully take 1st waffle omelet out from the waffle maker, then set it aside. Respray the waffle maker, then pour in leftover mixture. Let it bake for 3 to 4 minutes.
- Top using Avocado & salsa if you want.

Nutrients: Calories: 101kcal, Carbs: 1g, Protein: 8g, Fat: 7g

6. Keto & Low-Carb Lean and Green Sweet Potato Pecan Muffins

Prep time: 10mins

Cook time: 20mins

Servings: 4

Lean: 0

Green: 0

Condiments: 2

Ingredients

- 1 cup of cold water
- 2 sachets of honey sweet potatoes Optavia select
- 2 sachets of spiced gingerbread Optavia essential
- 1/4 cup original unsweetened
- 1/3 oz chopped pecans
- 6 tablespoons of egg substitute liquid
- 1/2 cup of pumpkin pie spice
- 1/2 teaspoon of baking powder
- 1/2 teaspoon of vanilla extract
- 1 can cooking spray

Instructions

- Set the oven at 350°F.
- Cook honey sweet potatoes as directed on the box. Allow cooling a little.
- Mix cooked honey sweet potatoes with the other ingredients inside a bowl.
- Inside the muffin pan, distribute the mix among eight spaces. Sprinkle chopped pecans over the tops.
- For 20 mins, bake.

Nutrients: Calories: 160kcal, Carbs: 18g, Protein: 4g, Fat: 8g

7. French Toast Sticks

Prep time: 15mins

Cook time: 5mins

Servings: 2

Lean: 0

Green: 0

Condiments: 1

Ingredients

- 2 tablespoons of cream cheese low-Fat
- 2 sachets of cinnamon crunchy o's cereal Optavia essential
- 2 tablespoons of syrup sugar-free
- 1 can cooking spray

- 6 tablespoons of egg substitute liquid

Instructions

- In blender, process Cinnamon Crunchy O's Cereal in breadcrumb-like uniformity.
- In a bowl, pour the processed Cinnamon Crunchy O's, add cream cheese & liquid egg-substitute, then mix well till it produces a dough. Make the dough into six French toast pieces.
- Spray pan and heat on high heat; cook French toast until warm & lightly brown from both sides.
- Top with syrup.

Nutrients: Calories: 221kcal, Carbs: 26g, Protein: 4g, Fat: 11g

8. Asparagus & Crab Meat Frittata

Prep time: 8mins

Cook time: 30mins

Servings: 4

Lean: 1

Green: 3

Condiments: 3

Ingredients

- 2 lbs. of asparagus
- 2 1/2 tablespoons of olive oil, extra virgin
- 1 tsp of salt
- 2 teaspoons of sweet paprika
- 1/2 teaspoon of black pepper
- 4 cups egg substitute liquid
- 1 lb. of crabmeat
- 1/4 cup of basil
- 1 tablespoon of finely chopped fresh chives

Instructions

- Set the oven at 375°F.

- Asparagus should have its rough ends trimmed off and be sliced into bite-sized pieces. Add pepper, paprika, and salt, if desired.
- The asparagus should be gently sweated until soft in heated olive oil inside a pan, between 8 and 10 minutes.
- Add the basil, chives, and crab meat to a bowl while asparagus is boiling. Add the liquid egg replacement and carefully stir everything together.
- Gently whisk the crab & egg mixture together after carefully adding it to the pan containing cooked asparagus. Cook eggs until they begin to bubble up over medium heat.
- Re-bake the pan in oven for 15-20 more minutes. Serve hot.

Nutrients: Calories: 169kcal, Carbs: 5g, Protein: 16g, Fat: 9g

9. Kale, Tomato, & Goat Cheese Egg Muffins

Prep time: 11mins

Cook time: 49mins

Servings: 4

Lean: 1

Green: 3

Condiments: 1

Ingredients

- 1 cup of beaten egg whites
- 9 beaten eggs
- 1/4 cup of beaten Greek yogurt low-Fat
- 1/2 teaspoon of salt
- 1 can of cooking spray
- 2 oz. of cubed goat cheese
- 2 cups of chopped cherry tomatoes
- 10 oz of chopped kale frozen

Instructions

- Set the oven at 375°F.
- In a bowl, thoroughly combine the egg whites, eggs, Greek yogurt, salt and goat cheese.
- Cherry tomatoes & kale have been added.
- Distribute the mixture equally among 20-24 slots of two-slot standard muffin pans that have been gently oiled.
- When the center is set, and knife pushed into the center comes back clean, cook for 20-25 minutes.

Nutrients: Calories: 179kcal, Carbs: 1.2g, Protein: 10g, Fat: 14g

10. Maple Turkey Sausage Patties with Spaghetti Squash Hash Browns

Prep time: 24mins

Cook time: 36mins

Servings: 4

Lean: 1

Green: 3

Condiments: 2

Ingredients

- 1 cup of chopped scallions
- 1 spaghetti squash
- 1/2 teaspoon of garlic powder
- 1/4 teaspoon of salt
- 3 eggs
- 1/2 teaspoon of black pepper
- 1/4 teaspoon of dried thyme
- 4 oz shredded cheddar cheese low-Fat
- 2 tsp. of olive oil
- 1/4 teaspoon of salt
- 2 teaspoons of olive oil
- 1/4 teaspoon of black pepper
- 1/2 teaspoon of dried sage
- 1/4 teaspoon of nutmeg

- 2 tablespoons of maple syrup sugar-free
- 1/4 teaspoon of rosemary
- 1 lb. of lean ground turkey

Instructions

- Get spaghetti squash ready. Discard the stringy pulp & seeds by cutting squash in two pieces.
- Every spaghetti squash half should be placed face down inside a baking dish that can be used into a microwave. Add approximately 1-inch water to the dish. For 10-15 minutes on high in the microwave.
- Make patties of turkey sausage while spaghetti squash is simmering. Inside a bowl, mix all the spices. With your hands, season the turkey with the syrup and spices. Patties made from the turkey mixture should be formed, and they should be cooked completely and gently browned in an oil-based pan.
- Use a fork to dig the spaghetti squash's meat into spaghetti-like strands, then cut the strands away from the skin. Let the squash chill before squeezing it several times in your hands on sink to drain the extra water.
- The strands of drained squash, garlic powder, scallions, salt, pepper and eggs should all be combined in a big basin.
- Stirring regularly, cook the squash combination in a pan using olive oil on moderate heat for 10-15 minutes.
- Cheddar cheese should be added right away. Maple turkey sausage patties should be served alongside.

Nutrients: Calories: 330kcal, Carbs: 37g, Protein: 40g, Fat: 13g

11. Broccoli Cheddar Breakfast Bake

Prep time: 10mins

Cook time: 45mins

Servings: 4

Lean: 1

Green: 3

Condiments: 2

Ingredients

- 9 eggs
- 6 cups of broccoli florets
- 1/4 teaspoon of cayenne pepper
- 4 oz shredded cheddar cheese reduced-Fat
- 1 cup almond milk unsweetened
- 1/4 teaspoon of black pepper
- 1 can cooking spray light

Instructions

- Set the oven at 375°F.
- Add broccoli and two to three tablespoons of water to dish. 3-4 mins on high in the microwave. To drain out any extra liquid, transfer the broccoli to a strainer.
- Until then, combine the eggs, milk, and spices in a dish.
- In baking dish that has been lightly oiled, arrange broccoli on bottom. After covering the broccoli with a layer of cheese, add the egg mix.
- Bake the dish for 40-45 minutes.

Nutrients: Calories: 232kcal, Carbs: 32g, Protein: 9g, Fat: 11g

12. Keto & Low-Carb Lean and Green Spinach & Pepper Jack Breakfast Burrito

Prep time: 15mins

Cook time: 10mins

Servings: 2

Lean: 1

Green: 3

Condiments: 3

Ingredients

- 4 egg whites
- 2 eggs
- 2 tablespoons of flax seeds whole
- 4 oz. of pepper shredded jack cheese reduced-Fat
- 3-dash cooking spray light
- 2 cups chopped baby spinach
- 1/2 cup of diced green bell peppers
- 1 cup of tomatoes diced
- 1 diced jalapeno peppers
- 1 teaspoon of minced garlic cloves
- 1/4 cup chopped Cilantro fresh
- 1 tablespoon of chopped red onion
- 1/8 teaspoon of salt
- 2 teaspoons of balsamic vinegar
- 1/8 tsp of black pepper

Instructions

- Mix tortilla's components in a bowl. A small pan should be heated over moderate flame and lightly greased using cooking spray. Add two eggs, four egg whites, plus two tablespoons whole flax seeds.
- In order to create a thin, tortilla- or crepe-like shape, put half the egg mix in the pan and spin to spread the eggs over surface evenly.
- The tortilla should be cooked for a few minutes till bottom & edges are crisp. Ensure the eggs aren't runny by tilting the pan from side to side. Using a spatula, gently pry the tortilla off surface and turn it over.
- Cook the eggs more until they are completely set. Repetition is required with the remaining tortilla mixture. When completed, put the tortillas aside.
- In same pan that has been lightly greased, cook the spinach on medium heat for 2-3 mins. Remove the heat when finished, then place aside.
- In a bowl, mix all the salsa's components. (bell pepper, diced tomatoes, red onion, jalapenos, garlic, salt, balsamic vinegar, pepper and Cilantro)

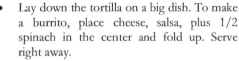
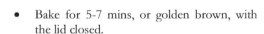
- Lay down the tortilla on a big dish. To make a burrito, place cheese, salsa, plus 1/2 spinach in the center and fold up. Serve right away.

Nutrients: Calories: 350kcal, Carbs: 19g, Protein: 29g, Fat: 17g

13. Lean and green cheddar and chive savory mashed potato waffles

Prep time: 8mins

Cook time: 7mins

Servings: 4

Lean: 3

Green: 1

Condiments: 2-3

Ingredients
- 1/2 cup of almond milk, unsweetened
- 1/4 cup of Greek yogurt low-Fat
- 4 sachets of smashed garlic creamy potatoes
- 1/2 cup of cheddar cheese reduced-Fat shredded
- 2 chopped turkey bacon
- 1/2 cup of egg substitute
- 1 can of cooking spray
- 1/4 cup of scallions chopped

Instructions
- Combine garlic creamy, smashed potatoes, cheese, milk, and egg replacement in a moderate mixing basin until fully incorporated.
- 2 slices turkey bacon, cooked as directed on the package, chopped into tiny pieces.
- Put the scallions diced.
- Fold all of ingredients together. Pour the batter on a waffle iron that has been lightly oiled and heated.

- Bake for 5-7 mins, or golden brown, with the lid closed.
- Take waffles out from waffle iron with care & serve.

Nutrients: Calories: 127kcal, Carbs: 17g, Protein: 5g, Fat: 4g

14. Lean and green eggnog

Prep time: 10mins

Cook time: 0mins

Servings: 1

Lean: 1

Green: 2

Condiments: 2

Ingredients
- 1 pinch of nutmeg
- 8 oz of vanilla almond milk unsweetened
- 1 sachet of creamy vanilla shake
- 8 oz of cashew milk
- 1/8 tsp. of rum extract
- 1 egg

Instructions
- Mix Optavia creamy vanilla shake, vanilla almond\cashew milk and 1/8 or 1/4 teaspoon rum extract, based on the strength of the rum flavor.
- Then, in a mixer, combine one egg yolk and mix until smooth.
- Whisk egg whites till firm peaks form inside stand mixer bowl.
- Spoon the shake solution over the top of egg mixture white inside a glass.

Nutrients: Calories: 200kcal, Carbs: 25g, Protein: 9g, Fat: 5g

15. Lean and green blondies of cinnamon bun

Prep time: 5mins

Cook time: 20mins

Servings: 4

Lean: 1

Green: 0

Condiments: 2

Ingredients
- 1/2 tsp. of cinnamon
- 4 sachets of cream cheese cinnamon swirl cake
- 1/2 tsp. of baking powder
- 2/3 cup of cashew milk
- 2/3 cup of vanilla almond milk, unsweetened
- 2 tbsp. of butter melted, unsalted
- 11/3 oz. of pecans chopped
- 1/2 tsp. of vanilla extract
- 3 tbsp. of egg substitute
- 1 can of cooking spray
- 1-2 packets of sugar substitute zero-calorie
- 1/4 cup of cream cheese

Instructions
- Preheat the oven at 350 degrees Fahrenheit.
- Combine the cinnamon, cinnamon cream cheese swirl cake, & baking powder inside a mixing basin.
- Stir in the butter, milk, and 2 tbsp egg whites till just mixed.
- Pecans should be folded in at this point. Pour the batter into a bread loaf pan that has been oiled.
- Mix vanilla extract, sugar substitute, cream cheese, and the leftover 1 tbsp of egg white in a mixing bowl till thoroughly blended.

- Swirl the cream cheese mix into the batter using a knife. Bake for 18–20 minutes.

Nutrients: Calories: 200kcal, Carbs: 27g, Protein: 1g, Fat: 9g

16. Red velvet lean and green pies

Prep time: 10mins

Cook time: 20mins

Servings: 4

Lean: 3

Green: 0

Condiments: 2

Ingredients
- 2 sachets of chocolate chip cookie
- 2 sachets of chip pancakes
- 1/2 tbsp. of cocoa powder unsweetened
- 1/2 cup of vanilla almond milk unsweetened
- 1-2 packets of sugar substitute, zero-calorie
- 1/2 tsp. of baking powder
- 1/2 cup of cashew milk
- 1 tsp. of apple cider vinegar
- 6 tbsp. of egg substitute
- 2 dash food coloring, red
- 1/2 cup of cream cheese, low-Fat
- 1 can of cooking spray

Instructions
- Preheat the oven at 350 degrees Fahrenheit.
- In a moderate mixing bowl, mix golden pancakes, cocoa powder, chewy chocolate chip cookies, & baking powder.
- Mix in the egg, milk, & apple cider vinegar till a batter-like formation is achieved.
- Add a smidgeon of red food coloring if desired.

21

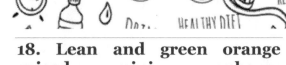
- Divide the mixture equally among 8 slots in a standard-shaped muffin tray that has been gently oiled. Cook for 15–20 minutes.
- Mix cream cheese & sugar substitute when the muffins start baking. After the muffins have cooled, cut them in half horizontally.
- 1 tbsp cream cheese mixture on base half of every muffin, followed by the other muffin halves.

Nutrients: Calories: 83kcal, Carbs: 12g, Protein: 1g, Fat: 3g

17. Lean and green peanut butter bites

Prep time: 5mins

Cook time: 0mins

Servings: 1

Lean: 1

Green: 0

Condiments: 0

Ingredients1
- 1 tbsp. of water
- 2 tbsp. of peanut butter, powdered
- 1 bar peanut butter creamy double crisp bar

Instructions
- In a bowl, mix the powder of peanut butter with water to make a paste.
- Heat creamy double butter peanut crisp bar for about 15secs.
- To make a dough, mix the heated bits of bar using peanut butter.
- Form 4 bite-sized balls using cookie scoop.
- Place in the refrigerator till ready to serve.

Nutrients: Calories: 200kcal, Carbs: 16g, Protein: 6g, Fat: 13g

18. Lean and green orange spiced mini cranberry cheesecake

Prep time: 9mins

Cook time: 1mins

Servings: 4

Lean: 1

Green: 0

Condiments: 2

Ingredients
- 1 1/2 cups of Greek yogurt, low-Fat
- 1 tsp. of orange zest
- 4 sachets of cranberry nut honey chili bars
- 2 tbsp. of cheesecake pudding, sugar-free

Instructions
- Using 8 cupcake liners, muffin tray.
- Every honey chili cranberry nut bar should be cut in half.
- Microwave the bar halves crunchy side down onto a microwave-safe tray for 20-30 seconds.

Nutrients: Calories: 409kcal, Carbs: 40g, Protein: 3g, Fat: 15g

19. Chocolate and peanut butter lean and green donuts

Prep time: 5mins

Cook time: 15mins

Servings: 4

Lean: 3

Green: 0

Condiments: 2

Ingredients

- 2 packets of double chocolate brownie
- 2 packets of chocolate chip pancakes
- 6 tbsp. of egg substitute
- 1/4 cup of cashew milk
- 1/4 cup of vanilla almond milk unsweetened
- 3-4 tbsp. of cashew milk
- 1/2 tsp. of vanilla extract
- 1 can of cooking spray
- 1/2 tsp. of baking powder
- 3-4 tbsp. of vanilla almond milk unsweetened
- 1/4 cup of peanut butter powder

Instructions

- Preheat the oven at 350 degrees Fahrenheit.
- Remove the Choco-chip pancakes from the sifter.
- Mix pancakes, liquid egg replacement, brownies, milk, baking powder and vanilla extract in a mixing dish.
- Divide the ingredients equally among the 4 slots of pan doughnut and bake for 12-15 minutes, or until the mixture is formed.
- Allow it to cool completely before glazing. Make the butter glaze when the doughnut is baking.
- Mix powder of peanut butter with milk in a shallow bowl till smooth & slightly runny. Every doughnut should be dipped in the glaze then topped using chocolate chips.

Nutrients: Calories: 360kcal, Carbs: 43g, Protein: 3g, Fat: 19g

20. Lean and green mint cookies

Prep time: 10mins

Cook time: 16mins

Servings: 4

Lean: 2

Green: 0

Condiments: 1

Ingredients

- 2 bars of cookie crisp chocolate mint bars
- 2 sachets of double chocolate brownie
- 1/4 tsp. of mint extract
- 1 tbsp. of egg substitute
- 2 tbsp. of cashew milk
- 2 tbsp. of almond milk unsweetened

Instructions

- Preheat the oven at 350 degrees Fahrenheit.
- Soften chocolate mint cookie crisp bars in the microwave for about 15-20 seconds.
- Combine the liquid egg replacement, decadent double chocolate brownies, milk, and mint essence in a mixing bowl.
- Microwave crunch bars should be added at this point.
- On a baking sheet, form the batter into eight pieces. Preheat oven to 350°f and bake for about 12-15 minutes.

Nutrients: Calories: 216kcal, Carbs: 9g, Protein: 3g, Fat: 15g

21. Lean and Green Eggs with Vegetable and Tofu Bowl

Prep Time: 10mins

Cook Time: 23mins

Servings: 4

Lean: 2

Green: 3

Condiments: 2

Ingredients

- 1/2 tsp. of Salt

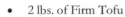
- 2 lbs. of Firm Tofu
- 1/2 tsp. of Black Pepper
- 1 cup of Cauliflower Florets
- 2 tsp. of Canola Oil
- 2 cups of Button Mushrooms
- 1 cup of diced Yellow Squash
- 2 tbsp Parmesan Cheese Low Fat
- 1 diced Red Bell Pepper
- 1 cup of diced Roma tomatoes
- 2 minced Garlic Cloves
- 11/2 tbsp. of minced Ginger Root
- 11/2 tbsp Soy Sauce Reduced Sodium
- 4 Eggs
- 1 tsp. of Sriracha
- 1/2 cup of Cilantro crushed

Instructions

- Cut the tofu into cubes after patting it dry.
- Sprinkle with salt, if desired.
- Heat the 2 tablespoons oil in a wok on moderate flame and fry the tofu on both sides till golden brown; put aside.
- In a wok, combine the mushrooms, cauliflower, squash, peppers, ginger, garlic, tomatoes, soy sauce, water and sriracha. Boil on high heat with the tofu on top.
- Lower heat to medium and cook for 12-15 minutes, stirring occasionally. Lower heat to low and, using a large spoon or scoop, scoop out all of the veggies and tofu in 4 serving dishes, dividing evenly.
- Carefully crack an egg in the leftover boiling liquid, making sure they don't break.
- Cook for five min on low heat.
- Take the eggs out from liquid with slotted spoon and place one egg on every vegetable & tofu dish.
- Pour an approximately equal quantity of cooking liquid on every dish and stir.
- Serve immediately with parmesan cheese sprinkled on top of every bowl.

Nutrients: Calories:376 kcal, Carbs:41 g, Protein:25 g, Fat:14 g

22. Waffle Maker Lean and Green Omelet

Prep Time: 5mins

Cook Time: 5mins

Servings: 1

Lean: 1

Green: 3

Condiments: 2

Ingredients

- 2 tbsp. of chopped Red Bell Peppers
- 6 tbsp. of Egg Substitute
- 2 tbsp. of chopped Onion
- 2 dashes of Cooking Spray
- 1 tsp. of chopped Jalapeno Peppers
- 1 tbsp. of Raw chopped Spinach
- 1 tbsp. of Salsa
- 1/4 Avocado cubed

Instructions

- Stir egg whites, bell pepper, spinach, onion, & jalapeño in a mixing bowl & thoroughly combine. This mixture should be able to pour into the waffle machine.
- Coat the top & bottom of the waffle maker using cooking spray before pouring in half of the batter. It must be enough to coat the bottom part softly.
- Allow 3-5 min for waffle maker to cook; if necessary, heat for an extra minute.
- Remove the first waffle omelet from the waffle maker with care and put it aside.
- Re-spray the waffle maker, then pour in the rest of the batter.
- Allow for another 3-4 minutes of cooking time, plus one extra minute if necessary.
- If preferred, top over Avocado & salsa.

Nutrients: Calories: 141kcal, Carbs: 2g, Protein: 12g, Fat: 8g

Chapter no. 3 Slider Recipes

1. Goat's Cheese and Pumpkin Salad

Prep Time: 5mins

Cook Time: 5mins

Servings: 4

Lean: 1

Green: 1

Condiments: 2

Ingredients
- 20 g Pumpkin seeds
- Oil spray
- 750 g Pumpkin
- 120 g Rocket
- 2 tbsp Olive oil
- 75 g Goat's cheese
- 1 tbs Balsamic vinegar

Instructions
- Preheat the oven to 200 degrees Celsius.
- Arrange the pumpkin inside a baking pan. Sprinkle with salt after lightly spraying with oil.
- Bake for about 25 mins.
- Cook for another 20 minutes.
- Meanwhile, roast seeds inside a dry frying pan on moderate heat for 1 to 2 minutes.
- In a dish, toss the pumpkin with the rocket.
- Crumble the cheese on top. In a bowl, whisk together the oil & vinegar, then season using pepper and salt.
- To serve, spread dressing on salad, then top with seeds.

Nutrients: Calories: 202kcal, Carbs: 19g, Protein: 6g, Fat: 12g

2. Hummus with Pumpkin Roasted Beetroot Salad

Prep Time: 20mins

Cook Time: 35mins

Servings: 8

Lean: 1

Green: 3-4

Condiments: 2

Ingredients
- 750 g Beetroot, peeled
- 1000 g unpeeled Kent pumpkin
- 2 tbsp Olive oil
- One 400g can of Canned chickpeas
- 1 tbsp Lemon juice
- 1 crushed Garlic clove
- Oil spray
- 1 tbs Tahini
- 4 sliced Radish
- ¼ cup flat-leaf parsley
- ¼ cup Fresh mint

Instructions
- Preheat the oven to 200 degrees Celsius.
- Using the baking paper, line two large baking pans.
- Place the pumpkin and beets on the trays that have been prepared.
- Add salt & pepper, then drizzle with oil. Bake for 30 to 35 minutes.

- Meanwhile, inside a stick blender, blend 1\2 olive oil, chickpeas, tahini, lemon juice, & garlic until nearly smooth. 2 tbsp.
- Piping hot water. Repeat until the mixture is completely smooth.
- salt & pepper to taste.
- Cover the bottom of a serving platter with hummus. Beets, pumpkins, & radishes go on top.
- Drizzle the leftover olive oil over the mint & parsley.

Nutrients: Calories: 211kcal, Carbs: 33g, Protein: 21g, Fat: 32g

3. Roasted Kale, Pumpkin, & Couscous Salad

Prep Time: 5mins

Cook Time: 5mins

Servings: 1

Lean: 0

Green: 2

Condiments: 1

Ingredients
- 125 g Pumpkin
- 2 tbsp orange juice No added sugar
- ¼ cup Dry couscous
- 1 tbsp chopped Fresh coriander

- 1 cup Coleslaw

Instructions
- In a heatproof bowl, place the couscous.
- Add 1\4 cup hot water to the mix.
- Stir well, cover, and set aside for four minutes or till liquid is completely absorbed.
- To divide the grains, scrape them with the fork.
- Toss the couscous with the pumpkin, coriander, kale slaw, and lemon juice.
- salt & pepper to taste. Serve.

Nutrients: Calories: 254kcal, Carbs: 32g, Protein: 7g, Fat: 7g

4. Cooked Kumara Salad with Roasted Capsicum, Green Beans, & Mustard Seeds

Prep Time: 15mins

Cook Time: 25mins

Servings: 4

Lean: 1

Green: 3

Condiments: 2

Ingredients
- 250 g Green beans
- 450 g Orange sweet potato
- 1 tsp ground cumin
- 2 tsp Mustard seeds
- ½ tsp Ground coriander
- 1 tbsp Olive oil
- 1 tbsp Lemon juice
- Oil spray
- 1 tsp Honey
- ½ cup Fresh coriander
- 150 g Roasted capsicum

Instructions

- Preheat the oven to 200 degrees C.
- Using baking paper, prepare a baking pan.
- Spray the sweet potato liberally with oil & place it on the prepared tray.
- Bake for 25 to 30 minutes. Steam beans for 3mins.
- Drain and rinse with cold water to refresh. Drain.
- In a frying pan on moderate heat, toast mustard seeds.
- Heat for one minute, stirring constantly, or till aromatic and seeds begin to pop.
- Stir in the cumin & coriander to mix.
- In a mixing bowl, add the spice combination, oil, lemon juice, and honey.
- Combine sweet potato, capsicum, beans, and coriander in a mixing bowl.
- Season with salt and pepper and mix lightly to incorporate.

Nutrients: Calories: 422kcal, Carbs: 50g, Protein: 17g, Fat: 13g

5. Heirloom Feta and Mint with Tomato Salad

Prep Time: 10mins

Cook Time: 0mins

Servings: 8

Lean: 0

Green: 2

Condiments: 1

Ingredients
- 4 Tomatoes
- 2 tsp Olive oil
- 800 g Cherry tomatoes
- 40 g feta cheese Reduced fat
- ½ cup Fresh mint

Instructions

- Place the tomato & mint mixture on a plate.
- Sprinkle with oil and top with the feta. To garnish, sprinkle with pepper and salt.

Nutrients: Calories: 265kcal, Carbs: 30g, Protein: 7g, Fat: 11g

6. Hazelnuts with Green Salad

Prep Time: 15mins

Cook Time: 10mins

Servings: 4

Lean: 1

Green: 3

Condiments: 2

Ingredients
- 2 tsp Olive oil
- 30 g Hazelnuts
- 1½ tsp Lemon juice
- 30 g parmesan cheese Shaved
- 1crushed Garlic clove
- ½ tsp Dijon mustard
- 2 Zucchini
- 2 Fennel bulbs
- 2 Celery
- 2 Rocket cups

Instructions
- Preheat the oven to 200 degrees Celsius.
- Bake the hazelnuts for 7 to 8 minutes. Chop coarsely.
- In a jug, combine the oil, mustard, juice, cold water and garlic.
- salt & pepper to taste. In a mixing basin, combine zucchini, fennel, Celery, and rocket.
- Toss in the dressing to mix. Combine the parmesan & hazelnuts in a mixing bowl.
- Serve with celery leaves & fennel fronds that have been saved.

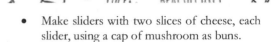
Nutrients: Calories: 59kcal, Carbs: 2g, Protein: 1g, Fat: 5g

7. Mushroom Bun Lean and Green Sliders

Prep Time: 15mins

Cook Time: 15mins

Servings: 4

Lean: 2

Green: 2

Condiments: 1

Ingredients

- 1/4 cup of diced Scallions
- 1 lb. of Ground Beef
- 1 tbsp. of Soy Sauce Reduced Sodium
- 2 cups of Romaine Lettuce
- 1 tbsp. of Worcestershire Sauce
- 1/2 tsp. of Garlic Powder
- 1 can of Cooking Spray
- 1/2 tsp. of salt
- 6 sliced Swiss Cheese Reduced-fat
- 12 caps of Portobello Mushroom
- 3 sliced Roma tomatoes

Instructions

- In a mixing bowl, mix the beef, Worcestershire sauce, scallions, garlic powder, soy sauce, and salt.
- Make 12 tiny beef patties with the ingredients, indenting one surface of the patties with your thumb.
- Spray the grill rack gently.
- Add the meat patties on the grill, then cover, and cook on moderate flame until done to your liking.
- Heat for 1-2mins each side on a grilling rack with cut mushroom caps.
- Every cheese slice should be cut into 4 pieces.

- Make sliders with two slices of cheese, each slider, using a cap of mushroom as buns.
- Garnish with lettuce & tomato slices.

Nutrients: Calories: 641kcal, Carbs: 24g, Protein: 52g, Fat: 40g

8. Taco Stuffed Lean and Green Portabellos

Prep Time: 10mins

Cook Time: 15mins

Servings: 4

Lean: 2

Green: 3

Condiments: 2

Ingredients

- 1 lb. of Lean Beef
- 4 caps of Portobello Mushroom
- 2 tbsp of onion chopped
- 1 minced Garlic Cloves
- 4 oz Cheddar Cheese Reduced-Fat spiraled
- 1/4 cup of diced Poblano Peppers
- 1 can of Tomatoes Diced
- 1 tsp. of Chili Powder
- 1 tsp. of Cumin
- 1/2 tsp. of Dried Parsley
- 1/4 tsp. of Black Pepper
- 1/4 tsp. of salt

Instructions

- Preheat the broiler to a low setting.

- Cut the stems & scrape the gills off the bottom of the mushrooms cap, discarding them. Place the mushrooms on a cooking pan and brush with olive oil.
- Broil for 4-5 minutes or until tender.
- Next, sear the beef inside a large pan with the pepper, onion, and garlic on moderate flame.
- Reduce the heat to low, add the tomatoes & seasonings, and continue to cook for ten min.
- Scoop one piece of the mix into every mushroom cap after dividing the mix into four halves.
- On the top of every mushroom, sprinkle cheese.

Nutrients: Calories: 340kcal, Carbs: 11g, Protein: 33g, Fat: 18g

9. Lean and Green Beef Pot Stickers Cabbage Wrapped

Prep Time: 10mins

Cook Time: 15mins

Servings: 1

Lean: 1

Green: 2

Condiments: 3

Ingredients

- 8 oz of Lean Beef
- 8 leaves of Green Cabbage
- 1 can of Cooking spray
- 2 tbsp. of chopped Green Onions
- 1/2 tsp. of Sesame Oil
- 1 3/4 tsp. of Soy Sauce Low Sodium
- 1/8 tsp. of Ground Ginger
- 1/8 tsp. of Garlic Powder

Instructions

- A big pot containing water should be brought to a boil.
- Boil the cabbage leaves inside a pot of water.
- Boil it for two min.
- Move cooked cabbage onto paper towels for draining using a slotted spoon.
- To make the pot-sticker filling, mix beef, sesame oil, green onions, ginger, soy sauce, & garlic powder inside a large mixing bowl.
- Make thick circular patties around the length of your finger to make the pot stick.
- Heat patties for 4mins on every side onto a nonstick skillet sprayed using cooking spray.
- Cooked patties should be wrapped in cabbages and secured with toothpicks.

Nutrients: Calories: 37kcal, Carbs: 4g, Protein: 5g, Fat: 0.6g

10. Lean and Green Club Tacos

Prep Time: 5mins

Cook Time: 2mins

Servings: 1

Lean: 2

Green: 2

Condiments: 1

Ingredients

- 2 slices of Cooked chopped Turkey Bacon
- 3 oz. of Grilled chopped Chicken Breast
- 1/2 Avocado diced
- 1 can of Cooking spray
- 1/2 cup of Diced Tomatoes
- 2 tbsp. of Ranch Reduced Fat
- 3 slices of milk provolone 2%
- 2 cups of chopped Romaine Lettuce

Instructions

- Place provolone cheese onto a paper plate greased with nonstick spray.

- Heat for 60sec on high heat. Remove the cheese from the microwave as soon as possible and, if required, reconstruct it into a circle.
- Allow five seconds to cool before shaping it into a taco shell.
- Allow it to cool completely before serving. Repeat with the remaining two cheese pieces.
- To complete the filing, follow these steps: Toss together the chicken, bacon, Avocado, tomatoes, lettuce and ranch dressing. Put lettuce mixture into the chilled taco shells.

Nutrients: Calories: 300kcal, Carbs: 7g, Protein: 5g, Fat: 6g

11. Lean and Green Burgers Jalapeno Cheddar

Prep Time: 10mins

Cook Time: 14mins

Servings: 4

Lean: 3

Green: 1

Condiments: 2

Ingredients

- 2 tbsp. of diced Onion
- 26 oz of Lean Beef
- 1/4 tsp. of salt
- 3 tbsp. of Cream Cheese Low Fat
- 1 tbsp. of Olive Oil
- 1/4 tsp. of Black Pepper
- 2 oz shredded Cheddar Cheese Low Fat
- 1 diced Jalapeno Peppers
- 1/4 tsp. of Garlic Powder

Instructions

- Preheat the grill to moderate.

- Mix the cheddar cheese, cream cheese, chopped jalapeño and garlic powder in a small mixing bowl.
- Combine the salt, meat, pepper, and chopped onion in a mixing bowl.
- Cut the meat into four equal pieces.
- Flatten a quarter of the mixture of cream cheese into a shape of pancake.
- Wrap the turkey/beef all-around cheese, ensuring that the cheese mix is well coated.
- Spray every burger using olive oil to prevent it from adhering to the grill.

Nutrients: Calories: 80kcal, Carbs: 0g, Protein: 5g, Fat: 6g

12. Quest Chips Taco Lean and Green Salad

Prep Time: 5mins

Cook Time: 7mins

Servings: 1

Lean: 1

Green: 1

Condiments: 2

Ingredients

- 1/2 tsp. of Taco Seasoning Mix Reduced Sodium
- 4 oz of Lean Beef
- 1.5 oz of Avocado sliced
- 1/3 cup of chopped Roma tomatoes
- 1 packet of Tortilla Taco Chips
- 1 3/4 cup of shredded Romaine Lettuce

Instructions

- Brown lean minced beef in a skillet.
- Return the meat to skillet after draining it. Heat for about 2-3 minutes after adding taco spice.
- Set aside and chill after reheating.

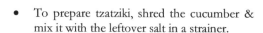
- Hand-shred, the lettuce, then tossed it into the dish with chopped tomatoes.
- Combine the prepared ground beef with the other ingredients.
- Additional condiments or Quest protein chips may be added to the salad.

Nutrients: Calories: 518kcal, Carbs: 18g, Protein: 33g, Fat: 38g

13. Lean and Green Greek Broiled Burger and Lettuce Wraps

Prep Time: 10mins

Cook Time: 20mins

Servings: 4

Lean: 1

Green: 3

Condiments: 2

Ingredients
- 1/2 tsp. of salt
- 11/4 lbs. of Lean Beef
- 2 tsp. of Garlic Cloves
- 1/2 tsp. of Black Pepper
- 1 stalk of Scallions minced
- 8 Romaine Lettuce
- 3 oz Crumbled Feta Low-fat
- 1 tbsp. of Capers minced
- 1/2 cup of Greek Yogurt Low-fat
- 11/4 lbs. of English Cucumbers

Instructions
- Combine the meat, half salt, pepper, and smashed garlic in a mixing bowl.
- Mix in the scallions & capers well. Incorporate in the crushed feta with a spatula, then form beef mixture in 8 patties and put aside.

- To prepare tzatziki, shred the cucumber & mix it with the leftover salt in a strainer.
- Allow 10mins for the cucumbers to dry in the strainer.
- Squeeze extra liquid from cucumbers.
- Toss the cucumbers with the yogurt, remaining pepper, & garlic, and mix to incorporate.
- Broil the beef burgers patties for 5min on high, turning once to ensure equal cooking & browning.
- Serve the burgers using tzatziki on a big lettuce leaf.

Nutrients: Calories: 238kcal, Carbs: 7g, Protein: 24g, Fat:13 g

14. Cumin Bistec Tacos Lean and Green

Prep Time: 10mins

Cook Time: 20mins

Servings: 4

Lean: 0

Green: 2

Condiments: 2

Ingredients
- 2 tbsp. of Lime Juice
- 2 lbs. of chopped Top Round Roast
- 1/2 tbsp. of Cumin
- 1 cup of Cilantro chopped
- 1/4 tsp. of Black Pepper
- 1/4 tsp. of salt
- 8 sliced Radishes
- 1 Jicama sliced

Instructions
- Top circular roast should be chopped or minced, and lime juice, salt, cumin, and pepper should be added.

- Add the meat to a nonstick pan that has been lightly oiled and heated on high.
- Let the beef color on single side prior to stirring, then add the sautéed meat and heat until it is fully done.
- Serve the meat in jicama tortillas & add Cilantro and sliced radishes.

Nutrients: Calories: 366kcal, Carbs: 6g, Protein: 32g, Fat: 11g

15. Bibimbap Bowls Lean and Green

Prep Time: 9mins

Cook Time: 11mins

Servings: 4

Lean: 1

Green: 3

Condiments: 3

Ingredients

- 5 cups of Baby Spinach
- 1 tsp. of Olive Oil
- 1 tsp. of Toasted Sesame Oil
- 1 lb. of Lean Beef
- 1/4 tsp. of salt
- 1 tbsp. of Sesame Seeds
- 2 tbsp. of Chili Garlic Sauce
- 2 cups Riced Cauliflower
- 1 tbsp. of Soy Sauce Reduced Sodium
- 1 cup sliced Cucumber
- 1/2 cup of chopped Green Onions
- 4 Eggs

Instructions

- In a pan, heat olive oil on moderate flame.
- Heat for several minutes or till the spinach is barely wilted.
- Pour sesame oil on top, then season gently with salt.

- Remove the spinach from the pan and put it aside. In the same pan where the spinach was cooked, add ground beef. Cook the steak until it has completely browned.
- Cook for 1 minute after adding the soy sauce and chili garlic sauce, then remove pan from heat. In a microwave-safe bowl, steam your riced cauliflower using 1 tablespoon water until soft, approximately 3-4 minutes.
- To make the bowls, start by putting half a cup riced cauliflower in everyone.
- Place 1/4 of each of the following ingredients on top: ground beef, spinach, and cucumber.
- In each dish, crack an egg and top using green onions & sesame seeds.

Nutrients: Calories: 972kcal, Carbs: 155g, Protein: 36g, Fat: 22g

16. Mac Salad Lean and Green

Prep Time: 5mins

Cook Time: 10mins

Servings: 1

Lean: 1

Green: 1

Condiments: 3

Ingredients

- 5 oz of Lean Beef
- 2 tbsp. of diced White Onions
- 2 tbsp. of Light Thousand Wish-Bone Island Dressing
- 1/8 tsp. of Onion Powder
- 1/8 tsp. of White Vinegar
- 1 tsp. of Sesame Seeds
- 3 cups of shredded Romaine Lettuce
- 1 oz sliced Dill Pickle
- 2 tbsp Cheddar Cheese Reduced-Fat

Instructions

- On moderate flame, gently oil a skillet.
- Cook, stirring occasionally, till the onion is aromatic, approximately 2 to 3 minutes.
- Heat until the meat is completely browned.
- Combine the vinegar, dressing, & onion powder in a mixing bowl.
- To assemble, follow these steps: Place the ground beef on top of the lettuce, then top using cheese.
- Serve with slices of pickle on top.
- Sprinkle with sauce & sesame seeds to finish.

Nutrients: Calories: 207kcal, Carbs: 26g, Protein: 3g, Fat: 9g

17. Burgers with Herb-Feta Sauce

Prep Time: 4mins

Cook Time: 20mins

Servings: 4

Lean: 3

Green: 2

Condiments: 2

Ingredients

- ¼ cup feta cheese crumbled
- 1 cup Greek yogurt nonfat
- 3 tablespoons of fresh oregano, chopped
- 2 teaspoons of lemon juice
- 1 sliced plum tomato
- ¼ teaspoon of lemon zest
- ¾ teaspoon of salt
- 1 pound of ground lamb
- 1 red onion
- ½ teaspoon of ground pepper
- 1 cup cucumber sliced
- 2 pitas, whole-wheat

Instructions

- Preheat the grill medium-high.
- In a bowl, combine yogurt, oregano, feta, lemon juice, lemon zest, and salt.
- In a mixing bowl, combine the chopped onion & meat and oregano salt and pepper.
- Form Four oval patties, each measuring approximately four inches by three inches.
- 4-6 minutes each side, grill the burgers, flipping once.
- Serve with sauce, cucumber, onion slices and tomato in pita halves.

Nutrients: Calories: 375kcal, Carbs: 23g, Protein: 29g, Fat: 18g

18. Lamb Rack with Lentil Salad and Warm Apple

Prep Time: 15mins

Cook Time: 25mins

Servings: 4

Lean: 2

Green: 2

Condiments: 1

Ingredients

- 1 ½ teaspoons of olive oil extra-virgin
- 2 tablespoons of dry breadcrumbs
- 1 teaspoon of fresh rosemary, chopped
- ¼ teaspoon of ground pepper
- ¾ teaspoon of kosher salt
- 1 trimmed and Frenched lamb rack
- 2 chopped shallots
- 3 teaspoons of Dijon mustard
- 2 teaspoons of sherry vinegar
- 1 15-ounce can of lentils
- 2 stalks of Celery with chopped leaves
- 1 chopped Granny Smith apple
- 3/4 cup of chicken broth reduced-sodium

Instructions

- Preheat the oven at 450 degrees Fahrenheit.
- In a bowl, combine breadcrumbs, oil, rosemary, salt, and pepper.
- In an ovenproof pan, heat the oil on moderate flame. Sear the lamb, meat-side down, for approximately 1 1/2 mins, until brown.
- Flip meat over, then sprinkle mustard all over.
- On the mustard, distribute breadcrumb mixture.
- Place the pan inside the oven, then roast for 15-20 minutes.
- To preserve lamb warm, place it on a platter and cover it with aluminum foil.
- Bring the pan to a high heat setting.
- Cook, stirring frequently, for 1 minute or until shallots begin to soften, adding rosemary, salt, and pepper.
- In a mixing bowl, combine the lentils, Celery, apple, broth vinegar, as well as mustard.
- Cook, stirring periodically, until the liquid has reduced slightly & Celery and apple have softened, approximately 4 minutes.
- Serve the lamb chops over lentils in 8 pieces.

Nutrients: Calories: 268kcal, Carbs: 21g, Protein: 26g, Fat: 2g

19. Lean and Green Zucchini and Turkey Meatballs Noodles

Prep Time: 5mins

Cook Time: 5mins

Servings: 4

Lean: 1

Green: 1

Condiments: 1

Ingredients
- 4 Zucchini spiraled
- 2 tbsp of Olive Oil
- 1 lb. of Turkey Meatballs
- 1/4 cup of chopped Fresh Basil
- 1 cup of Rao's Homemade Sauce

Instructions
- Cook turkey meatballs according to package directions.
- In a pan, heat the olive oil on moderate flame.
- Put zucchini noodles into the hot olive oil and toss until softened, about 2-3 mins.
- Lower the heat and toss the zucchini noodles with Rao's Sauce.
- Allow 2 to 3 minutes for the sauce-noodle combination to boil.
- Before serving, combine the hot meatballs into a sauce-noodle combination and cook for 2 minutes.
- Serve using a basil garnish on top of each dish.

Nutrients Calories: 365.3kcal, Carbs: 28g, Protein: 30g, Fat: 14g

20. Sheet Pan Lean and Green Lettuce Wraps, Chicken Fajita

Prep Time: 15mins

Cook Time: 30mins

Servings: 2

Lean: 2

Green: 2

Condiments: 2-3

Ingredients

- 1/4 cup of Plain Greek Yogurt Non-Fat
- 2 julienned Green Bell Peppers
- 6 Romaine Lettuce
- 1 lb. sliced Skinless Boneless Chicken Breast
- 1/2 tbsp of Lime Juice
- 2 tsp of Olive Oil
- 2 tsp of Fajita Seasoning

Instructions

- Preheat the oven to 400 degrees Fahrenheit.
- In a big, zippered plastic bag, add all ingredients apart from lettuce.
- To uniformly cover the chicken and veggies with oil and spice, combine all ingredients in a large mixing bowl.
- Bake approximately 25-30 minutes, till chicken is cooked, after spreading the ingredients of the bag equally on a baking sheet.
- Put on lettuce pieces with a dollop of Greek yogurt on top if preferred.

Nutrients Calories: 402kcal, Carbs: 20g, Protein: 35g, Fat: 10g

21. Salmon with Cucumber, Tomato, and Dill Salad

Prep Time: 15mins

Cook Time: 15mins

Servings: 4

Lean: 1

Green: 1

Condiments: 2

Ingredients

- 2 cups of Cherry Tomatoes
- 4 cups sliced Cucumber
- 1 Lemon

- 1/4 cup of Apple Cider Vinegar
- 1/4 tsp of Black Pepper
- 1/4 tsp of salt
- 1 1/2 lbs. of Skinless Boneless Salmon fillets

Instructions

- Preheat the oven to 350 degrees Fahrenheit.
- To create the salad, stir the first five ingredients together in a mixing basin.
- Place the salmon on baking pan and season each side with Zaatar.
- Roast until the temperature reaches 145 degrees Fahrenheit.
- Salad & lemon wedges should be served with roasted Fish.

Nutrients: Calories: 418kcal, Carbs: 10g, Protein: 38g, Fat: 25g

22. Lean and Green Watercress & Roasted Eggplant with Grilled Tempeh

Prep Time: 10mins

Cook Time: 34mins

Servings: 4

Lean: 1

Green: 1

Condiments: 3

Ingredients

- 41/2 cup of Eggplant
- 20 oz of Tempeh
- 1 tsp of Lime Juice
- 1/2 tsp of Black Pepper
- 1/2 tsp of Rice Vinegar
- 1/2 tsp of salt
- 1/4 cup of Scallions diced
- 1 1/2 cups of Watercress
- 11/2 tbsp of Soy Sauce Reduced Sodium
- 1/2 tbsp of Lemon Juice

Instructions

- Allow it for 30 minutes of soaking by pouring boiling water on the Tempe to cover this by 2 inches.
- Combine the Eggplant, pepper, rice vinegar, and salt in a mixing bowl.
- Preheat the oven at 425°F, then roast Eggplant for 20-30 minutes.
- Take the cooked Eggplant out from the oven, then combine with the scallions, Watercress, lemon juice, tomatoes, and a quarter tsp right away.
- Take the tempeh out from water and wipe it with a paper towel.
- It should be sliced into 1/4-inch pieces.
- 2 mins on every side, grill sear sliced tempeh till golden brown.
- Drizzle soy sauce & lime juice over the cooked tempeh over eggplant salad.

Nutrients: Calories: 310kcal, Carbs: 20g, Protein: 28g, Fat: 16g

23. Quest Chips Lean and Green Taco Salad

Prep Time: 5mins

Cook Time: 7mins

Servings: 1

Lean: 1

Green: 1

Condiments: 2

Ingredients

- 1/2 tsp of Taco Seasoning Mix Reduced Sodium
- 4 oz of Lean Beef
- 1.5 oz of sliced Avocado
- 1/3 cup of chopped Roma tomatoes
- 1 packet Tortilla Style Taco Chips
- 1 3/4 cup shredded Romaine Lettuce

Instructions

- Brown your lean minced beef in a skillet.
- Place the meat in skillet after draining it. Heat for about 2-3 minutes after adding taco spice.
- Set aside and chill after reheating.
- Hand-shred the lettuce and toss it into the dish with chopped tomatoes.
- Combine the prepared ground beef with the other ingredients. Optional condiments or Quest protein chips may be added to the salad.

Nutrients: Calories: 313kcal, Carbs: 16g, Protein: 32g, Fat: 15g

24. Shrimp Campechana Lean and Green Salad

Prep Time: 15mins

Cook Time: 15mins

Servings: 4

Lean: 1

Green: 4

Condiments: 3

Ingredients

- 1 lb. of whole Tomatoes
- 2 lbs. of Raw Shrimp
- 1 Garlic Cloves
- 1 chopped Jalapeno Peppers
- 2 stalks of Scallions
- 1 tsp Oregano Dried
- 1/2 tbsp of Olive Oil
- 8 Green Olives
- 1/2 cup of Cilantro chopped
- 1/4 tsp of Black Pepper
- 4 tbsp of Lime Juice
- 1 Avocado diced
- 1/4 tsp of salt
- 2 1/2 cup of Romaine Lettuce

Instructions

- Preheat the oven. Boil the water, then cook the shrimp for 2-3 minutes.
- Remove the shrimp and place them in an ice bucket. Set aside after draining and patting dry.
- In a bowl, combine the jalapeño, tomatoes, garlic, & scallions.
- Broil for 5-10 minutes on a sheet pan. Remove the pan from the oven and set it aside to cool completely.
- Remove the core of the tomatoes, the stem of the jalapeño, the peel of the garlic, and the root of the scallions.
- Place all ingredients in a blender and blend until finely chopped.
- Fill a mixing dish halfway with the tomato mixture.
- Toss in the olives, Cilantro, lime juice, Avocado, & shrimp. Sprinkle with salt and pepper.
- Pour the dressing over the lettuce, then serve.

Nutrients: Calories: 350kcal, Carbs: 14g, Protein: 48g, Fat: 12g

25. Mini Mac Lean and Green Salad

Prep Time: 5mins

Cook Time: 10mins

Servings: 1

Lean: 2

Green: 0

Condiments: 2

Ingredients

- 5 oz of Lean Beef
- 2 tbsp of diced White Onions
- 1 tsp of Sesame Seeds
- 2 tbsp of Wish-Bone Light Thousand Island Dressing
- 1/8 tsp of Onion Powder
- 1/8 tsp of White Vinegar
- 3 cups of Romaine Lettuce shredded
- 1 oz sliced Dill Pickle
- 2 tbsp of Cheddar Cheese Reduced-Fat

Instructions

- Over moderate flame, gently oil a skillet.
- Cook, stirring occasionally, until onion is aromatic, approximately 2-3 minutes.
- Cook till the meat is completely browned.
- Combine the vinegar, dressing, & onion powder in a mixing bowl.
- To assemble, place ground beef on top of the lettuce, then top with cheese.
- Serve with slices of pickle on top. Sprinkle with sauce & sesame seeds to finish.

Nutrients: Calories: 69kcal, Carbs: 7g, Protein: 3g, Fat: 3g

26. Tuna Nicoise Lean and Green Salad

Prep Time: 10mins

Cook Time: 0mins

Servings: 4

Lean: 1

Green: 2

Condiments: 1

Ingredients

- 3 tbsp of Balsamic Vinegar
- 4 tsp Olive Oil Extra Virgin
- 2 minced Garlic Cloves
- 1/8 cup of sliced Red Onion
- 2 cups of steamed String Beans
- 6 cups of Mixed Greens
- 1 cup of Grape Tomatoes

- 2 cans of Tuna drained
- 6 hard-boiled Eggs
- 3 pitted Black Olives

Instructions

- Combine the balsamic vinegar, olive oil, and garlic in a mixing bowl.
- Prepare a mixed greens bed.
- Boiled green beans, sliced hard-boiled eggs, half tomatoes, black olives, red onion, and Tuna are layered on top of each other.
- Drizzle the oil mixture over top.

Nutrients: Calories: 405kcal, Carbs: 18g, Protein: 39g, Fat: 13g

27. Lean and Green Swai Fish Lemon Pepper with Parmesan Garlic Asparagus

Prep Time: 5mins

Cook Time: 10mins

Servings: 4

Lean: 2

Green: 1

Condiments: 2

Ingredients

- 3 pinch Cooking Spray
- 1 sliced Lemon
- 1 1/2 lbs. of Swai Fish
- 2 tsp of salt-free Lemon Pepper Seasoning
- 1/4 cup of grated Parmesan Cheese
- 1/2 tsp of salt
- 1 1/2 lbs. of Asparagus
- 1/2 tsp of Garlic Powder

Instructions

- Preheat the oven at 400 degrees Fahrenheit.
- In a lightly oiled, foil-lined baking sheet, put the Swai fish.

- Using cooking spray, coat the surface of Swai fish, season using lemon pepper spice and salt, if preferred, and garnish using lemon slices.
- Mix parmesan cheese & garlic powder inside a bowl.
- Spray liberally with cooking spray & place asparagus spears all around Swai fish.
- Toss asparagus with a combination of parmesan cheese & garlic powder.
- Bake for 15-20 minutes.

Nutrients: Calories: 302kcal, Carbs: 2g, Protein: 24g, Fat: 22g

28. Rainbow Salad

Prep Time: 5mins

Cook Time: 0mins

Servings: 1

Lean: 1

Green: 2

Condiments: 1

Ingredients

- 2 cups red cabbage (shredded)
- 2 cups green cabbage (shredded)
- 2 carrots (julienned)
- 3 sliced green onions
- 1/3 cup apple juice concentrate
- 2 celery stalks (sliced)
- 1 chopped apple
- 1/2 cup tofu mayo
- 1 tbsp. lemon juice

Instructions

- Inside a salad dish, combine the carrots, cabbage, Celery, & green onions.
- Toss the apple with the lemon juice inside a separate dish. Toss with salad.
- Mix in the apple juice extract and tofu mayo.

Nutrients: Calories: 39kcal, Carbs: 8g, Protein: 1g, Fat: 0.4g

29. Easy and Healthy Salad Recipes

Prep Time: 5mins
Cook Time: 0mins
Servings: 1
Lean: 1
Green: 2
Condiments: 2

Ingredients

- 1 cup of microgreens
- 4 cups of arugula
- Champagne Vinaigrette
- 6 ounces of smoked salmon
- 1 sliced pear
- 1 1/2 sliced avocado
- 1 tomato cut in cubes
- salt & pepper
- 1/2 sliced red onion

Instructions

- In a bowl, combine all the components and sprinkle using Champagne Vinaigrette.
- Toss together everything gently & serve right away.

Nutrients: Calories: 300kcal, Carbs: 15g, Protein: 10g, Fat: 23g

Chapter no. 4 Lunch Recipes

1. Lean and Green Chicken and Tzatziki with Cauliflower Pizza

Prep Time: 10mins

Cook Time: 50mins

Servings: 4

Lean: 3

Green: 1

Condiments: 1

Ingredients
- 2 Eggs
- 5 half cups of Riced Cauliflower, Frozen
- 1 tablespoon of Parmesan Cheese, Low-fat
- 1 lb. of sliced Chicken Breast
- 1/4 tsp of Salt
- 10 Kalamata Olives
- 1/4 tsp of Black Pepper
- 1/2 tsp of Garlic Cloves
- 1/2 tsp of Italian Seasoning
- 1 cup reduced-fat mozzarella cheese
- 1/2 cup of Plain Greek Yogurt Non-Fat
- 1/2 cup of cucumber grated

Instructions
- Preheat oven to 425 degrees Fahrenheit. Bake cauliflower rice till golden brown.
- Allow it to cool. Squeeze your cauliflower in a kitchen towel to absorb any extra liquid.
- Combine cauliflower, parmesan cheese, eggs, and salt in a mixing bowl; stir.
- Put the cauliflower ingredients on a baking sheet & form this into a 12-inch pizza-shaped circle.

- In a bowl, add olives, chicken strips, pepper, and Italian seasoning, and toss to combine.
- Place chicken strips and also olives on the cauliflower crust, and sprinkle using mozzarella cheese, then bake at 425-degree F for 20 minutes till golden brown.
- When the crust of cauliflower pizza is baking, tzatziki sauce must be made.
- Mix the grated yogurt, cucumbers, garlic and salt.
- Cut cauliflower pizza into four wedges, then top every wedge using tzatziki.

Nutrients Calories: 324kcal, Carbs: 12g, Protein: 37g, Fat: 16g

2. Chicken Crust Lean and Green Veggie Pizza

Prep Time: 15mins

Cook Time: 15mins

Servings: 2

Lean: 3

Green: 2

Condiments: 1

Ingredients
- 1 Egg
- 1 cup of Baby Spinach
- 1 1/2 cups of sliced Tomatoes
- 2 tbsp of Grated Parmesan
- 1/3 cup of sliced Onions
- 1/3 cup of chopped Bell Peppers
- 1/2 tsp of Italian Seasoning
- 1/2 lb. of Lean Chicken Ground
- 1/2 cup of Mozzarella Cheese Reduced-Fat

- 1/3 cup of sliced White Mushrooms

Instructions

- Oven 400F. In a medium bowl, combine chicken egg, parmesan, and also Italian seasoning.
- Prepare a baking sheet with the chicken mixture.
- Bake 20 minutes till browned.
- Add spinach, mozzarella, sliced tomatoes, and your choice of vegetable toppings on the crust of chicken. 7–10 minutes till cheese is warmed.
- Serve in 4 equal-sized pieces.

Nutrients Calories: 240kcal, Carbs: 4g, Protein: 14g, Fat: 25g

3. Thai Curry Lean and Green Coconut Chicken

Prep Time: 10mins

Cook Time: 5mins

Servings: 1

Lean: 2

Green: 2

Condiments: 2

Ingredients

- 1/4 cup of Scallions
- 1 tsp of Sesame Oil
- 2 tsp of Paste of Red Curry
- 1/3 cup of lite milk coconut
- 2.75 cups of Cauliflower, Cooked
- 1/8 tsp of Garlic Powder
- 1 tsp of Fish Sauce
- 1 dash Salt
- 2 tbsp of chopped Cilantro
- 18 oz of cubed Skinless Boneless Chicken Breast

Instructions

- Remove the whites & greens of the scallions.
- Heat the oil in a nonstick pan over.
- Sauté for 1 minute with the scallion whites & red curry paste.
- Cook till nearly done with garlic powder, diced chicken, and salt.
- Mix in the coconut milk & fish sauce. Simmer for 2 to 3 minutes.
- Remove the pan from the heat and stir in the scallion greens & cilantro.
- Serve on cauliflower rice that has been cooked.

Nutrients Calories: 354kcal, Carbs: 9g, Protein: 19g, Fat: 31g

4. Crock-Pot Lean and Green Creole Chicken

Prep Time: 15mins

Cook Time: 180mins

Servings: 4

Lean: 3

Green: 2

Condiments: 1

Ingredients

- 1 cup of Leeks
- 4 9-oz Skinless Boneless Chicken Breast
- 2 minced Garlic Cloves
- 1 14.5-oz. tin of Diced Tomatoes Low Sodium
- 1 quarter cup of Chicken Broth Low Sodium
- 1 cup of Green Onions
- 1 tbsp of Tomato Paste
- 1/4 tsp of Cayenne Pepper
- 2 tsp of Creole seasoning
- 1 Bell Peppers. Green

Instructions

- Except for the green onions, combine all of the ingredients inside the crockpot.
- Heat on high heat for three hours, covered.
- Cook the creole and shred the chicken to your preferred texture.
- Green onions should be placed on top of each dish.

Nutrients Calories: 189kcal, Carbs: 13g, Protein: 29g, Fat: 2g

5. Grilled Chicken Lean and Green Tomato Bruschetta

Prep Time: 20mins

Cook Time: 6mins

Servings: 4

Lean: 1

Green: 2

Condiments: 1

Ingredients
- 2 minced Garlic Cloves
- 3 chopped Tomatoes Vine Ripe
- 2 tbsp of basil chopped
- 36 oz Chicken Breast
- 4 tsp Olive Oil Extra Virgin
- 1/4 cup of finely chopped Red Onion
- 1 tbsp of Balsamic Vinegar
- 1/2 tsp of Black Pepper
- 1/4 tsp of salt

Instructions
- Combine olive oil, red onions, balsamic vinegar, salt, and pepper in a mixing bowl.
- Place the tomatoes in a mixing basin, chopped. Add salt and pepper to the garlic, onion, basil, & balsamic vinegar mixture.
- Set aside for at 10 minutes to allow the flavors to meld. Preheat grill coat the grates using vegetable oil to prevent them from sticking.

- Season the raw chicken using pepper and salt.
- Cook the chicken for approximately 2-3 mins.
- After the chicken breasts have finished grilling, transfer them to a platter and top each using tomato bruschetta.

Nutrients Calories: 282kcal, Carbs: 7g, Protein: 38g, Fat: 11g

6. Slow Cooker Lean and Green Salsa Chicken

Prep Time: 10mins

Cook Time: 135mins

Servings: 7

Lean: 2

Green: 1

Condiments: 1

Ingredients
- 1 1/4 cups of Salsa
- 1 Fresh Cilantro
- 6 9-oz Skinless Boneless Chicken Breast
- 1 can of Cooking spray
- 1 cup of Mexican Cheese Blend Reduced-Fat

Instructions
- Place the entire chicken in a cooker and top with salsa. Heat on high for 1-2 hours.
- Cooking the chicken much longer will cause it to come apart.
- After cooking, set the salsa aside. Preheat the oven to 425 degrees Fahrenheit.
- Use an 8x8 or 9x13 baking sheet. Before placing the chicken, coat the pan with nonstick spray.
- Over chicken, pour some of the remaining salsa and equally distribute the cheese.

- Bake for about 15 minutes, and bubble with sauce & cheese.
- If desired, top with a sprinkling of cilantro.

Nutrients Calories: 230kcal, Carbs: 6g, Protein: 39g, Fat: 4g

7. Lean and Green Spinach Pizza & Chicken Alfredo

Prep Time: 10mins

Cook Time: 40mins

Servings: 1

Lean: 4

Green: 2

Condiments: 0

Ingredients
- 1/4 cup of Egg Beaters
- 1 cup of cauliflower grated
- 1 can of Cooking spray
- 1/2 cup of shredded Mozzarella Cheese Reduced-Fat
- 1/2 cup of Spinach
- 21/4 oz of chopped Chicken Breast Cooked
- 2 slices of Light Garlic & Herb Cheese Wedges
- 2 tsp grated Parmesan Cheese Reduced-Fat
- 2 tbsp of Half and Half

Instructions
- Preheat the oven. Grease a cookie sheet. Mix up the egg beaters, grated cauliflower, and mozzarella cheese.
- Spoon the mixture onto a parchment-lined cookie sheet.
- Thin out the material using a spoon. Bake for thirty min.
- Turn over the crust and bake for another 10 minutes.
- Alternatively, wait until it looks to be finished and then put it away.

- Cut 2.25 oz roasted chicken breast, then combine mozzarella cheese and spinach in a mixing bowl.
- Garlic & Herb Cheese Wedges, grated parmesan in a saucepan. Cook, stirring regularly, till the sauce is bubbling and thickened on moderately low heat.
- Mix in the chicken after removing the pan from heat.
- Set aside. Spread the cooked spinach on top of the crust.
- Then, on the spinach, spoon the chicken combination.
- Mozzarella cheese is sprinkled over the top.
- You may add other toppings like chopped tomatoes and olives.
- Just till the cheese melts, broil pizza. Keep an eye on the pizza to avoid it scorching.

Nutrients Calories: 387kcal, Carbs: 32g, Protein: 26g, Fat: 17g

8. Lean and Green Chicken Cauliflower Enchiladas

Prep Time: 5mins

Cook Time: 20mins

Servings: 2

Lean: 2

Green: 1

Condiments: 0

Ingredients
- 6 oz of Raw chopped Chicken Breast
- 2 Cauliflower Tortillas
- 1 Ancho Chile Pepper Dried
- 1 can of Cooking Spray
- 1 Garlic Cloves
- 1/2 tsp of Chicken Bouillon
- 2 tsp Mozzarella divided Low-fat
- 1/3 cup of shredded Mozzarella Low-fat

Instructions

- Make big cuts in the uncooked chicken.
- Put in a pot & cover using water; come to one boil, cover for 10-15 minutes, or until cooked completely.
- When chicken is done, slice it using a fork and put it aside.
- While the chicken is cooking, boil the ancho chili pepper in water for about ten min in a separate small pot.
- Take the pepper out from water after ten min and put it aside to chill.
- Keep the water that was used for cooking the peppers.
- Remove the stem & inner seeds of pepper flesh after it has cooled. Puree the pepper flesh, boiling liquid, garlic clove and chicken bouillon in a food processor or blender till smooth.
- For enchiladas, gently spray a pan. In a pan, heat the sauce that was produced in the food processor.
- Cauliflower tortilla should be submerged in sauce and turned over once with a heat-safe utensil.
- After the tortilla has been soaked on both sides, transfer it to a platter and top it with chicken & cheese; roll the tortilla on the dish.
- Replace chicken, cauliflower tortilla, and cheese with the leftover chicken, cauliflower tortilla, and cheese.

Nutrients Calories: 311 kcal, Carbs: 3g, Protein: 33g, Fat: 18g

9. Crock-Pot Lean and Green Chicken Parmesan

Prep Time: 5mins

Cook Time: 280mins

Servings: 4

Lean: 2

Green: 2

Condiments: 1

Ingredients

- 2 cups of Crushed Tomatoes
- 2 tbsp of grated Parmesan Cheese Reduced-Fat
- 4 (6oz.) oz of Skinless Boneless Chicken Breast
- 1/2 tsp of Italian Seasoning
- 1/2 tsp of Onion Powder
- 3/4 tsp of Basil
- 2 Garlic Cloves

Instructions

- Preheat the slow cooker on high.
- In crock cooker, place four chicken breasts.
- In a mixing bowl, combine the tomatoes, basil, Italian seasoning, onion powder, parmesan cheese and garlic.
- On the chicken breast, spoon the sauce.
- Cook for six to eight hours on low.
- Half a cup of sauce should be served with every chicken breast.

Nutrients Calories: 475kcal, Carbs: 27g, Protein: 50g, Fat: 17g

10. Lean and Green Shrimp Gumbo and Chicken

Prep Time: 20mins

Cook Time: 30mins

Servings: 3

Lean: 3

Green: 3

Condiments: 1-2

Ingredients

- 1 Scallion chopped
- 1 tbsp of Canola Oil

- 2 stalks of celery diced
- 2 cups of Water
- 1.5 cups of Diced Tomatoes
- 1 Bay Leaf
- 1/4 tsp of Dried Thyme
- 1/4 tsp of Cayenne Pepper
- 1 diced Red Bell Pepper
- 1 lb. Skinless Boneless Chicken Thighs
- 1.5 cups of okra chopped
- 2 cups Riced Cauliflower Frozen
- 1/4 tsp of Salt
- 3/4 lbs. of Raw Shrimp
- 1/4 tsp of Black Pepper

Instructions

- In a saucepan, heat the oil & add the scallions, garlic, bell pepper, and celery sauté until the scallions, garlic, celery, & bell pepper are translucent.
- Boil for fifteen min after adding the tomatoes, thyme, water, cayenne and bay leaf.
- Continue to cook for another 10 minutes after adding the okra and chicken.
- Boil for 3 minutes before adding the cauliflower & shrimp.
- If the gumbo is excessively thick, thin it out with water as needed.
- Season to taste with pepper and salt, and serve immediately.

Nutrients Calories: 267kcal, Carbs: 17g, Protein: 41g, Fat: 3g

11. Arroz Con Pollo Lean and Green

Prep Time: 10mins

Cook Time: 30mins

Servings: 4

Lean: 1

Green: 3

Condiments: 0

Ingredients

- 1/4 tsp of Salt
- 1 3/4 lbs. of Skinless Boneless Chicken Breast
- 1 1/2 cups of Green Beans
- 1/4 tsp of Black Pepper
- 1 stalk of Scallions minced
- 2 minced Garlic Cloves
- 4 cups of Riced Cauliflower Frozen
- 40 pitted Green Olives
- 1 1/2 cups of Cherry Tomatoes

Instructions

- Preheat the oven.
- Season the chicken with pepper and salt.
- Roast the chicken in oven for approximately 20mins.
- Remove the chicken breasts from the oven and lay them aside.
- In a saucepan, add all of the other ingredients and the chicken cooks.
- Boil for 8 - 10 mins on low heat. When the chicken is done, slice it, then serve it over cauliflower rice.

Nutrients Calories: 556kcal, Carbs: 35g, Protein: 30g, Fat: 33g

12. Crock-Pot Lean and Green Spinach & Artichoke Chicken

Prep Time: 15mins

Cook Time: 240mins

Servings: 6

Lean: 2

Green: 3

Condiments: 2-3

Ingredients

- 4 Garlic Cloves

- 2 tsp of Olive Oil
- 24 oz Skinless Boneless Chicken Breast
- 12 oz of Artichoke Hearts
- 1 cup of chopped leeks
- 2 cups of spinach chopped
- 1/4 cup of Water
- 1 tsp of Lemon juice
- 1/2 cup of Red Peppers Roasted
- 1 tsp of Dried Parsley
- 1 tsp of Chicken Bouillon
- 1 tsp of Dried Oregano
- 1 tsp Red Pepper Crushed Flakes
- 1 tsp of Basil
- 1 tsp of Black Pepper
- 1/2 tsp of salt

Instructions

- Olive oil, garlic cloves, and chicken breast in a skillet over medium.
- Cook the chicken for around three to four minutes on every side.
- Remove the chicken breasts from the package and put them in a crock cooker on high cooking for 4 hours.
- Leeks, artichoke hearts, spinach, and red peppers are sautéed till spinach is softened & onions are transparent in hot skillet where the chicken cooks.
- Place the mixture on the chicken breasts in the crock cooker.
- Water, chicken bouillon, parsley, oregano, basil, red pepper flakes, salt, black pepper, and lemon juice, whisked together and poured over the vegetables & chicken inside the crockpot.
- Boil for 4 hours on high.

Nutrients Calories: 548kcal, Carbs: 7g, Protein: 44g, Fat: 37g

13. Lean and Green Kohlrabi and Chicken Noodle Soup

Prep Time: 20mins

Cook Time: 30mins

Servings: 4

Lean: 3

Green: 1

Condiments: 2

Ingredients

- 2 tbsp of Soy Sauce Reduced Sodium
- 4 Eggs
- 21/2 lbs. of Kohlrabi
- 2 cups Chicken Broth Low Sodium
- 11/4 lbs. of Skinless, Boneless sliced Chicken Breast
- 1 tsp of Chili Oil
- 1/2 cup of Fresh Basil
- 2 stalks of chopped Green Onions
- 2 tbsp of Sesame Seeds
- 1/4 tsp of Red Pepper Flakes Crushed

Instructions

- In a saucepan, put the eggs and cover using water.
- Boil the water and then reduce to low heat for 6 minutes.
- Place the eggs in iced water to chill for ten min after they've been fried.
- Peel your eggs gently and put them inside a small bag.
- Add soy sauce to the bag and carefully squeeze out air.
- Allow 1 hour for the eggs to marinade. Let 30-60 minutes for the chicken to marinate in soy sauce. In a soup pot, heat the chicken stock to a boil.
- Combine the red pepper flakes, chicken and kohlrabi noodles in a large mixing bowl.
- Simmer for 3-5 minutes.
- Add basil leaves & scallions and mix well.
- Split the eggs in half after removing them from soy sauce.
- Fill 4 soup bowls with an equal quantity of noodles & chicken, then gently pour liquid.
- Garnish with eggs, chili oil and sesame seeds.

Nutrients Calories: 260kcal, Carbs: 15g, Protein: 42g, Fat: 14g

14. Lean and Green Eggplant Parmesan with Grilled Chicken

Prep Time: 10mins

Cook Time: 20mins

Servings: 4

Lean: 3

Green: 1

Condiments: 1

Ingredients

- 8 tsp of Flake Nutritional Yeast
- 6 tbsp of Almond Milk Unsweetened
- 1/4 tsp of Salt
- 1 lb. of eggplant sliced
- 1/4 tsp of Black Pepper
- 11/2 lbs. of sliced Skinless Boneless Chicken Breast
- 1 can Cooking Spray
- 2 minced Garlic Cloves
- 1 can of Diced Tomatoes
- 1/4 cup of chopped Fresh Basil
- 2 stalks of Scallions chopped

Instructions

- Preheat the oven at 400 degrees Fahrenheit.
- In a mixing bowl, mix almond flour, nutritional yeast, salt, and pepper.
- Wash the eggplant and slice it, coating both sides using almond flour mixture.
- Put eggplant pieces onto a baking sheet that has been gently oiled.
- Preheat oven to 350°F and bake for twenty minutes, turning halfway through.
- Inside a saucepan, mix the garlic, tomatoes, and scallions and cook on for 15-20 minutes when the eggplant bakes.

- Remove the eggplant from the oven after it's done cooking and garnish with tomato sauce & grilled chicken.

Nutrients Calories: 407kcal, Carbs: 12g, Protein: 35.3g, Fat: 24.4g

15. Lean and Green Chicken Potpie Cauliflower Crust

Prep Time: 17mins

Cook Time: 23mins

Servings: 4

Lean: 4

Green: 1

Condiments: 1

Ingredients

- 1/2 cup of Water
- 4 cups of Riced Cauliflower Frozen
- 1/4 cup of grated Parmesan Cheese
- 1 1/4 lbs. of cubed Skinless Boneless Chicken Breast
- 1 Egg
- 1/2 cup of celery drained
- 1/2 cup of quartered Button Mushrooms
- 1/2 cup of diced Kobacha Squash
- 1 cup Almond Milk Unsweetened
- 1/2 cup of Green Beans
- 1 cup of Chicken Broth
- 1-2 stalks of Fresh Thyme

Instructions

- Preheat the oven to 400 degrees Fahrenheit.
- In a bowl, combine cauliflower & water.
- 5mins in the microwave, or till cauliflower is soft.
- Drain the cauliflower and set it aside to cool.
- Drain as much water out of the cauliflower as you can using a cheesecloth.

- Combine parmesan cheese, riced cauliflower, and egg in a mixing bowl.
- Spread the cauliflower mix into four equal-sized circles onto a baking tray.
- Preheat oven to 400°F and bake the crust of cauliflower for 4-8mins, or until the center is dry & crust is nicely browned.
- To prepare the pot pie filling, combine the other ingredients and riced cauliflower in Instant Pot.
- Secure the cover, choose the meat/stew setting, and set the timer for 10 minutes.
- When the Instant Pot beeps, let the pressure out normally.
- Fill bowls halfway with chicken potpie contents and top using a cauliflower crust.

Nutrients Calories: 810kcal, Carbs: 86g, Protein: 26g, Fat: 40g

16. Lean and Green Cauliflower Buffalo Chicken Crust Pizza

Prep Time: 10mins

Cook Time: 50mins

Servings: 4

Lean: 3

Green: 2

Condiments: 0

Ingredients
- 3 Eggs
- 5 cups of Riced Cauliflower
- 3/4 tsp of Salt
- 1 cup of shredded Mexican Cheese Blend Reduced-Fat
- 2 tbsp of Hot Sauce
- 3/4 lbs. of shredded Rotisserie Chicken Breast
- 4 stalks of finely chopped Scallions
- 1 tsp of Garlic Powder
- 3 tbsp of cubed Blue Cheese Reduced-Fat

Instructions
- Preheat the oven at 425 degrees Fahrenheit.
- Bake cauliflower for about 30 minutes.
- Allow it to cool after removing it from the oven.
- Squeeze cauliflower into kitchen towel to eliminate excess liquid.
- Combine the eggs, cauliflower, and salt in a mixing bowl.
- Press cauliflower mixture into a 12" circle.
- Preheat oven to 400°F and bake until 8 min.
- Assemble the toppings when the dough bakes.
- In a mixing bowl, combine all the components except mozzarella cheese.
- Take the sheet pan out from the oven and distribute the assembled toppings equally over the top.
- On the top of those ingredients, sprinkle the appropriate quantity of mozzarella cheese, then cook pizza for 10-12 mins.
- Cut your pizza into eight pieces of similar size.

Nutrients Calories: 280kcal, Carbs: 20g, Protein:13g, Fat: 17g

17. Lean and Green Mediterranean Chicken Sheet Pan & Vegetables

Prep Time: 30mins

Cook Time: 15mins

Servings: 4

Lean: 2

Green: 3

Condiments: 1

Ingredients
- 3 Roma tomatoes
- 4 (8oz.) Skinless Boneless Chicken Breast

- 1 Zucchini sliced
- 1 Orange Bell Pepper
- 1 sliced Yellow Squash
- 1 tsp of Olive Oil
- 1 tbsp of Olive Oil
- 1/4 tsp of Salt
- 1/4 tsp of Black Pepper
- 4 tbsp of Feta Reduced-Fat
- 1 tsp of Dried Oregano
- 2 minced Garlic Cloves
- 2 tbsp of Lemon Juice

Instructions

- Preheat the oven. Spray a baking sheet with nonstick cooking spray.
- Arrange the chicken into a single layer.
- Combine the veggies, salt, oil, and pepper in a large mixing bowl. Separately from the chicken, move to the baking sheet on the other side of the baking sheet and place it in a thin layer.
- Bake for fifteen min on a baking sheet in the oven.
- To create the dressing, mix together the oregano, garlic, lemon juice, & olive oil inside a small bowl.
- Drizzle approximately 1 1/2 to 2 tablespoons of dressing over the top. Continue with the remaining three servings.

Nutrients Calories: 327kcal, Carbs: 26g, Protein: 30g, Fat: 11g

18. Lemon Chicken Lean and Green Spaghetti Squash with Spinach and Tomatoes

Prep Time: 15mins

Cook Time: 30mins

Servings: 4

Lean: 2

Green: 4

Condiments: 1-2

Ingredients

- 1/2 tsp of Salt
- 2 lbs. cubed Skinless Boneless Chicken Breast
- 1/2 tsp of Black Pepper
- 1/4 cup of diced Yellow Onion
- 4 cups of Spaghetti Squash
- 1 tbsp of Olive Oil
- 2 pt. minced Garlic Cloves
- 2 cups of Baby Spinach
- 1 cup of Cherry Tomatoes
- 1/2 cup of Lemon Juice
- 1 cup of Chicken Broth Low Sodium

Instructions

- Heat the oven to 400°F and bake the half spaghetti squash for approximately 20mins.
- Using 1/4 tsp salt and black pepper, season the chicken breasts.
- In a pan, heat the olive oil over moderate flame.
- Cook the chicken breasts in a skillet until they are cooked through, approximately 7-10 minutes.
- Removed the chicken from the pan and placed it on a plate.
- Sauté the onion & garlic in the pan for 1-2 minutes or until fragrant.
- Cook, stirring occasionally, until tomatoes start to soften, approximately 2-3 minutes.
- Lower the heat, add the lemon juice, chicken broth, and the extra salt, and simmer until the fluid is cut by half, approximately 15 minutes.
- Cook, stirring occasionally, until the spinach has wilted, approximately 2 minutes.
- Serve the contents of the pan over spaghetti squash that has been cooked.

Nutrients Calories: 489kcal, Carbs: 40g, Protein: 28g, Fat: 24g

19. Maple Turkey Lean and Green Sausage Patties and

Hash Browns of Spaghetti Squash

Prep Time: 24mins

Cook Time: 36mins

Servings: 4

Lean: 2

Green: 1

Condiments: 1

Ingredients

- 1 cup of Scallions chopped
- 1 Spaghetti Squash
- 1/2 tsp of Garlic Powder
- 1/4 tsp of Salt
- 3 Eggs
- 1/2 tsp of Black Pepper
- 4 oz shredded Cheddar Cheese Low-fat
- 2 tsp of Olive Oil
- 1/2 tsp of Dried Sage
- 1/4 tsp of Rosemary
- 2 tsp of Olive Oil
- 1/4 tsp of Dried Thyme
- 1/4 tsp of Nutmeg
- 1/4 tsp of Black Pepper
- 1/4 tsp of Salt
- 1 lb. of Lean Turkey Ground
- 2 tbsp of Maple Syrup Sugar-Free

Instructions

- Cook spaghetti squash according to package directions.
- Remove the stringy pulp and seeds from the squash by cutting them in half.
- Add 1 inch of water and place every spaghetti squash piece face down.
- Microwave for about 10-15 minutes. Make patties of turkey sausage while the spaghetti squash is simmering.
- In a mixing dish, combine all of the spices.
- With your hands, mix the spices and syrup into the ground turkey.
- Form patties from the turkey mixture and fry until heated through and gently browned in a pan using olive oil.
- Pull threads from the spaghetti squash and scratch the meat with a spoon to make spaghetti-like threads.
- Allow squash to cool before squeezing the strands in the hands a few times to drain any extra liquid.
- Drain scallions, squash strands, eggs, garlic powder, salt, and pepper in a large mixing basin.
- In a pan with olive oil, cook the squash mixture for approximately 10-15 minutes, turning constantly, until lightly browned.
- Serve immediately using patties of maple turkey sausage & cheddar cheese on top.

Nutrients Calories: 330kcal, Carbs: 37g, Protein: 40g, Fat: 13g

20. Shredded Beef Lean and Green Stew

Prep Time: 10mins

Cook Time: 35mins

Servings: 4

Lean: 1

Green: 3

Condiments: 0

Ingredients

- 2 shredded Garlic Cloves
- 1.5 lbs. of Flank Steak
- 4 cups of Riced Cauliflower
- 1 tsp. of Dried Oregano
- 1 tsp. of Smoked Paprika
- 1 tsp. of Cumin
- 1 Bay Leaf
- 1/4 tsp. of Salt
- 1 can of Diced Tomatoes
- 1/4 tsp. of Black Pepper
- 4 Green Olives
- 1 sliced Green Bell Pepper

Instructions

- Combine all of the ingredients, excluding the olives, bell peppers, & riced cauliflower.
- Secure the cover, set the Instant Pot to meat mode, then set the timer for 30 mins at elevated pressure.
- When the Instant Pot sounds, let the pressure out normally.
- Remove the cover and break the meat with two forks.
- Add the bell pepper & olives to the Instant Pot with the shredded meat. In the Instant Pot, put the cauliflower in the steamer basket. Heat for five min using steam mode.
- Inside a bowl, pour beef stew on the riced cauliflower.

Nutrients: Calories: 330kcal, Carbs: 14g, Protein: 38g, Fat: 13g

21. Mexican Meatloaf Lean and Green

Prep Time: 10mins

Cook Time: 65mins

Servings: 6

Lean: 4

Green: 0

Condiments: 1

Ingredients

- 1/2 cup of Egg Beaters
- 2 1/4 lbs. of Lean Beef
- 1 tsp. of Chili Powder
- 4 oz chopped Green Chilies
- 1/4 tsp. of Salt
- 1/2 tsp. of Cumin
- 2 minced Garlic Cloves
- 1 cup shredded Monterey Jack Cheese Reduced-Fat
- 1/2 cup of Salsa
- 1 cup shredded Cheddar Cheese Reduced-Fat

Instructions

- Preheat the oven to 375 degrees Fahrenheit.
- Combine the meat, eggs, and seasonings in a mixing bowl.
- Roll the ground beef mix into a thin square on waxed paper.
- Half of the cheese & green chili should be sprinkled on top.
- Wrap wax paper until it is fashioned in a loaf roll with the ends tucked up so that nothing leaks out.
- Remove the wax paper with care.
- Serve in a loaf pan and salsa on top.
- Preheat oven to 350°F and bake for 50-55 minutes.
- Top using cheese and bake for 10 minutes.

Nutrients: Calories: 170kcal, Carbs: 9g, Protein: 21g, Fat: 5g

22. Lean and Green Fajita Cauliflower Steak Crust Pizza

Prep Time: 7mins

Cook Time: 60mins

Servings: 4

Lean: 2

Green: 2

Condiments: 0

Ingredients

- 3 Eggs
- 5 cups of Riced Cauliflower
- 3/4 tsp. of Salt
- 1 cup shredded Mozzarella Cheese Reduced-Fat
- 1 cup sliced Green Bell Peppers
- 3/4 lbs. of Flat Iron Steak
- 1 tsp. of Cumin
- 1/4 cup of Tomatillo Salsa
- 1/2 tsp. of salt

Instructions

- Preheat the oven to 425 degrees Fahrenheit.
- Bake cauliflower for about thirty min on baking sheet.
- Allow it to cool after removing from the oven.
- Compress the cauliflower to eliminate excess liquid.
- Combine the eggs, cauliflower, & salt in a mixing bowl.
- Press the cauliflower mixture into a circle of 12 inches on sheet pan.
- Preheat oven to 400°F and bake for 8 minutes.
- Assemble the toppings when the crust bakes.
- Sprinkle the steak with salt and sear this on both sides over high temperature in a nonstick pan until nicely brown.
- Remove the pan from the heat and put it aside.
- In same pan, add the peppers, remaining salt, cumin, & tomatillo salsa, along with water, & cook for 2-3 minutes.
- Mix the cooked skirt steak, sautéed peppers, & salsa in thinly sliced cut against the grain.
- Take the sheet pan out from oven and distribute the assembled toppings equally over the top.

- Sprinkle the appropriate quantity of mozzarella cheese, and bake pizza about 400°F for 10-12 minutes.
- Divide the pizza in 8 equal pieces.

Nutrients: Calories: 119kcal, Carbs: 13g, Protein: 9g, Fat: 4g

23. Cheeseburger Soup Lean and Green

Prep Time: 10mins

Cook Time: 35mins

Servings: 4

Lean: 3

Green: 4

Condiments: 1

Ingredients

- 1/4 cup chopped Onion
- 1 lb. of Lean Beef
- 3/4 cup diced Celery
- 3 cups Chicken Broth Low Sodium
- 4 oz shredded Cheddar Cheese Reduced-Fat
- 1 can diced Tomatoes
- 1 tsp. of Dried Parsley
- 2 tsp. of Worcestershire Sauce
- 1/4 tsp. of Salt
- 7 cups of Baby Spinach
- 1/4 tsp. of Black Pepper

Instructions

- Cook the meat until it is brown in a soup pot. Sauté the onion & celery until they are soft.
- Remove the pan from the heat, then drain any remaining liquids.
- Combine the tomatoes, Worcestershire sauce, broth, parsley, pepper and salt in a large mixing bowl.
- Cover and cook for twenty minutes on low heat.

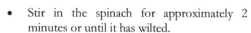
- Cook, stirring occasionally, till the spinach has wilted, approximately 1-3mins.
- Cheddar cheese should be placed on top of every dish.

Nutrients: Calories: 450kcal, Carbs: 33g, Protein: 19g, Fat: 27g

24. Keto and Low-Carb Italian Wedding Soup

Prep Time: 5mins

Cook Time: 15mins

Servings: 4

Lean: 3

Green: 2

Condiments: 1

Ingredients
- 1.25 lbs. of Lean Beef
- 6 cup Chicken Broth Low Sodium
- 4 oz. of Raw Spinach
- 1 Egg
- 1 tsp. of Italian Seasoning
- 1/4 cup of grated Parmesan Cheese
- 4 cups Riced Cauliflower
- 1/4 tsp. of salt

Instructions
- In a saucepan, heat half broth.
- In a mixing bowl, combine the meat, egg, parmesan cheese, Italian seasoning, & salt.
- Make tiny meatballs using the ingredients, approximately 1/2-inch in size.
- Add the meatballs to the liquid and heat for five min or until they are done through.
- Bring the remaining stock and Italian spice to a boil.
- Cook, stirring occasionally, until the cauliflower rice is soft, approximately 5 minutes.

- Stir in the spinach for approximately 2 minutes or until it has wilted.
- Serve the soup with the remaining parmesan cheese on top.

Nutrients: Calories: 303kcal, Carbs: 6g, Protein: 29g, Fat: 20g

25. Oregano and lemon Lamb Chops

Prep Time: 20mins

Cook Time: 15mins

Servings: 4

Lean: 0

Green: 2

Condiments: 1

Ingredients
- 1 tablespoon of chopped oregano
- 2 lemons zest
- 1 ¼ teaspoon of kosher salt
- 8 lamb loin trimmed chops
- 2 teaspoons of olive oil extra-virgin
- Ground pepper
- 1/4 cup of tahini
- ¼ cup seeded cucumber, diced peeled
- ¼ cup plain yogurt, nonfat
- 2 minced cloves garlic
- ¼ cup of lemon juice
- 1-3 tablespoons of water
- 1 tablespoon of fresh parsley chopped

Instructions
- Preheat the oven at 400 degrees Fahrenheit.
- In a bowl, combine the lemon zest, salt, oregano, and pepper.
- Spread the mixture all over the chops of lamb and put aside for about 10mins.
- In a mixing bowl, mix the yogurt, tahini, cucumber, garlic, lemon juice, parsley, and

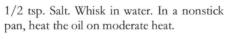
1/2 tsp. Salt. Whisk in water. In a nonstick pan, heat the oil on moderate heat.

- Cook for 2 minutes or till the chops of lamb is browned on a single side.
- Flip the pan on and place it in the oven.
- 8-14 mins, based on thickness, till a thermometer is placed into the chop, read 135 ° F. for moderate.
- With tahini sauce, offer the chops.

Nutrients: Calories: 269kcal, Carbs: 7g, Protein: 23g, Fat: 16g

26. Grilled Lamb Leg and Mint-Garlic Rub

Prep Time: 60mins

Cook Time: 60mins

Servings: 16

Lean: 1

Green: 1

Condiments: 1

Ingredients
- ½ cup parsley leaves flat-leaf
- 1 cup of fresh leaves of mint
- 3 cloves of garlic
- 1 5-pound of boneless lamb leg
- 2 teaspoons of kosher salt
- ¼ cup olive oil extra-virgin
- 1 teaspoon of ground pepper

Instructions
- Mint, garlic and parsley should all be finely chopped and combined in a basin.
- Combine the oil, salt, & pepper in a mixing bowl.
- Dry the lamb with a paper towel.
- Spread the herbs on the lamb in an equal layer.
- To enable the flavors to permeate, cover and chill for 3hrs or for 1 day.

- Take the lamb out from refrigerator approximately one hour before you are ready to grill.
- Preheat a moderate charcoal grill and move the embers to single side.
- Grill lamb on direct heat for 10-15mins each side.
- If meat is becoming too browned, transfer it to a cooler portion of grill every now and then.
- Place the lamb onto cutting board, cover with foil, then let aside for 10 mins before slicing.

Nutrients: Calories: 175kcal, Carbs: 0.9 g, Protein: 21g, Fat: 9g

27. Lemon-Garlic with Meatballs Orzo

Prep Time: 5mins

Cook Time: 35mins

Servings: 4

Lean: 2

Green: 2

Condiments: 3

Ingredients
- 1 egg
- 1 pound of ground lamb
- 4 tablespoons of fresh parsley, chopped
- 3 teaspoons of garlic, grated
- 1 tablespoon of fresh mint chopped
- ½ teaspoon of salt
- 1 cup sliced cucumbers
- 3 tablespoons of olive oil extra-virgin
- 1 cup orzo whole-wheat
- 2 tablespoons of fresh dill chopped
- ½ cup yogurt whole-milk
- Zest & juice 1 lemon
- 1 cup feta cheese, crumbled

Instructions

- Preheat the oven at 425 degrees Fahrenheit.
- Using cooking spray.
- In a mixing basin, combine the lamb, egg, parsley, mint, garlic, & salt. Make 12 balls, then set them on prepared baking sheet.
- Cook for approximately 20 minutes.
- In the meanwhile, boil the water.
- Cook orzo as directed on the packet.
- Drain and set aside for 5mins to cool.
- In a bowl, combine the oil, lemon zest, dill, & lemon juice, as well as parsley & garlic.
- In a dish, combine herb mixture, yogurt, and feta cheese.
- In a mixing bowl, combine the orzo as well as feta cheese.
- Toss the meatballs and orzo, cucumbers and yogurt sauce before serving.

Nutrients: Calories: 586kcal, Carbs: 37g, Protein: 32g, Fat: 35g

28. Lamb and Spinach Pasta

Prep Time: 15mins

Cook Time: 35mins

Servings: 5

Lean: 2

Green: 1

Condiments: 2

Ingredients

- 1 pound of ground lamb
- 8 ounces elbow noodles whole-wheat
- 6 cups of chopped spinach
- 1 onion, chopped
- 2 tablespoons of feta cheese crumbled
- 1 can diced tomatoes no-salt-added
- 2 tablespoons of tahini
- 4 sliced cloves garlic
- 1 teaspoon of ground cumin
- ¾ teaspoon of salt

- 1 teaspoon of dried oregano
- 4 cups of water

Instructions

- In a saucepan, combine the pasta, spinach, lamb, tomatoes, garlic, onion, tahini, oregano, cumin, and salt.
- Add the water and mix well.
- Over high temperature, boil it. Boil, stirring often, for 10-12 minutes.
- Take off the heat & let it aside for five min, stirring regularly.
- Serve with some feta cheese on top.

Nutrients: Calories: 400kcal, Carbs: 42g, Protein: 24g, Fat: 16g

29. Lamb Chops and Mint Pot Sauce

Prep Time: 20mins

Cook Time: 20mins

Servings: 4

Lean: 1

Green: 1

Condiments: 2

Ingredients

- 1 ½ teaspoons of cornstarch
- ⅓ cup of apple juice
- 8 chops of lamb loin
- ½ teaspoon of ground pepper
- ½ teaspoon of kosher salt
- 2 tablespoons of fresh mint, minced
- 1 teaspoon of canola oil
- ⅓ cup beef broth reduced-sodium
- 1 minced shallot
- 2 tablespoons of mint jelly
- 2 tablespoons of cider vinegar

Instructions

- Preheat the oven at 450 degrees Fahrenheit.

- In a dish, mix apple juice & cornstarch; leave aside.
- Season the chops of lamb with pepper and salt before serving.
- In ovenproof skillet, heat the oil on moderate flame. Cook for 2 mins.
- Turn the pan over and place it in the oven. Roast it for 6-10 minutes, according to thickness.
- Move the chops into a platter and cover with foil. Preheat the skillet on medium-high. Cook, stirring frequently, till shallot is caramelized & softened, approximately 1 minute.
- Heat the vinegar, broth, and jelly, stirring constantly to incorporate the jelly.
- Heat, whisking continually, for 2-3 minutes.
- Stir together the cornstarch & water, then add into pan and cook, stirring frequently, until sauce thickens, approximately 30 seconds.
- Take the pan out from heat and mix in half of the mint, as well as any remaining chop juices.
- Garnish the chops using the leftover mint & sauce on top.

Nutrients: Calories: 197 kcal, Carbs: 11g, Protein: 19g, Fat: 7g

30. Spinach Spaghetti

Prep Time: 10mins

Cook Time: 35mins

Servings: 4

Lean: 1

Green: 2

Condiments: 3

Ingredients
- 1 tsp Olive oil
- 5 peeled Eschalots

- 200 g soft tofu
- ⅓ cup flat-leaf parsley
- 1 tsp grated lemon rind
- 4 cups baby spinach leaves
- 2 tbsp Lemon juice
- 125 g quartered Cherry tomatoes,
- 250 g Legume pasta, spaghetti

Instructions
- Preheat the oven at 200 degrees Celsius.
- Wrap entire eschalots in tin, spray over oil, add salt & pepper, then cover in foil to cover.
- Bake for about thirty min on a baking pan.
- In a stick blender, puree the spinach, tofu, and parsley till smooth.
- Pulse in the lemon juice & toasted eschalots to mix.
- Salt & pepper to taste. Meanwhile, prepare pasta according to package directions in a large pot of boiling water till tender.
- Return to the same pan after draining.
- Stir in the tofu sauce on low flame to mix and cook through.
- For serving, divide the pasta across 4 dishes and top with parsley, tomatoes, and lemon peel.

Nutrients: Calories:182 kcal, Carbs:36 g, Protein: 6g, Fat: 1g

31. Moroccan (Chorba) Vegetable Soup

Prep Time: 30mins

Cook Time: 60mins

Servings: 6

Lean: 2

Green: 3

Condiments: 2

Ingredients

- 1 diced onion
- 2 tablespoons of olive oil extra-virgin
- 2 teaspoons of ground turmeric
- 6 cups of beef broth reduced-sodium
- 1 pound of stew beef meat
- 1 can of tomatoes diced
- 2 diced carrots
- 2 turnips
- 2 stalks of celery
- 12 sprigs of parsley, flat-leaf
- ½ teaspoon of ground pepper
- Saffron threads
- 8 sprigs of fresh Cilantro
- 2 ounces of angel hair pasta
- 1 peeled zucchini
- 1-2 teaspoons of salt

Instructions

- Heat the oil on moderate flame. Stir in the onion & turmeric until well combined.
- Cook, stirring regularly, for 4 mins. Add broth, tomatoes, turnips, tomato juice, celery, carrots, and saffron to the pot.
- Add the parsley & cilantro sprigs to your pot after tying them together along with kitchen string.
- Toss the soup inside a pot with enough water to cover it and boil.
- Lower heat and cover.
- Cook for 45-50 minutes.
- Cook and cover for 8-10 minutes. Cook, stirring occasionally, 4-10 minutes, based on the type of pasta.
- Remove the parsley & cilantro sprigs, then discard. Add salt & pepper. If desired, garnish using parsley & cilantro leaves.

Nutrients: Calories: 231kcal, Carbs: 18g, Protein: 20g, Fat: 8g

32. Balsamic-Marinated Lamb Leg

Prep Time: 20mins

Cook Time: 10hrs.

Servings: 12

Lean: 2

Green: 0

Condiments: 2

Ingredients

- 4-6 sliced cloves garlic
- 1 lamb leg, rolled and boned
- ⅔ cup of balsamic vinegar
- 2 tablespoons of Dijon mustard
- ½ cup of olive oil
- 4 basil or mint leaves
- 1 tablespoon of sugar
- 4 minced cloves garlic
- 2 teaspoons of crushed dried basil
- ½ teaspoon of ground pepper
- 1 teaspoon of salt

Instructions

- Trim any excess fat from the lamb.
- Slice pockets in the lamb, place a piece of garlic through each pocket.
- In a bowl, whisk together the oil, balsamic vinegar, mustard, basil, sugar, salt, pepper and minced garlic for the marinade.

- In a resealable plastic bag, put the lamb leg.
- Over the meat, pour marinade. Close the bag and flip the lamb to cover it.
- Marinate for 8 hours, inverting the bag regularly.
- The marinade should be drained and discarded.
- Preheat the oven to 325°F. Place the sheet on a rack inside a small roasting pan coated with foil. In thickest part of its leg, insert an oven-safe meat thermometer.
- Heat until desired level of doneness is reached.
- Allow 2 and a half to 3 hours for moderate doneness or 2-3 hours for moderate doneness.
- Before cutting, cover and set aside for fifteen min.
- Following standing, the lamb should be 145 degrees Fahrenheit. Strings must be removed. To serve, slices the lamb. Sprinkle with mint\basil, if preferred.

Nutrients: Calories: 188kcal, Carbs: 0.5g, Protein: 27g, Fat: 7.5g

33. Green Chili Lean and Green and Tomatillo Pork Stew

Prep Time: 25mins

Cook Time: 20mins

Servings: 4

Lean: 1

Green: 4

Condiments: 3

Ingredients
- 2 stalks of Scallions
- 2 Garlic Cloves
- 1 lb. of Tomatillos chopped
- 1 Romaine Lettuce
- 2 chopped Serrano Chilies

- 1/2 tsp. of Dried Oregano
- 1/4 tsp of Salt
- 4 Lime quartered
- 1 1/2 lbs. of Pork Loin Boneless
- 1/4 tsp of Black Pepper
- 1/4 cup of Radishes sliced
- 1/4 cup of cilantro chopped
- 1 sliced Jalapeno Peppers

Instructions
- In a mixer, purée the garlic, tomatillos scallions, serrano chilies, lettuce leaves, & oregano till smooth.
- In a saucepan, combine the pork & tomatillo mixture.
- If there isn't enough puree to cover the pork, then add water till it is.
- Season it with salt & pepper, then bring it to a low simmer.
- Simmer for 20 minutes on low heat.
- Garnish with radishes, cilantro, lettuce, jalapenos, & lime wedges after the stew is done simmering.

Nutrients: Calories: 231kcal, Carbs: 8g, Protein: 22g, Fat: 12g

34. Lean and Green Cauliflower Steak& Peri-Peri Pork

Prep Time: 15mins

Cook Time: 42mins

Servings: 4

Lean: 1

Green: 2

Condiments: 1

Ingredients
- 1 tsp of Canola Oil
- 4 Roma tomatoes
- 1 tbsp of Fresh Thyme

- 1/4 tsp of Salt
- 2 minced Garlic Cloves
- 1/4 cup of Fresh chopped Cilantro
- 1/4 tsp of Black Pepper
- 1 Head of Cauliflower
- 1 can of Cooking Spray
- 2 tbsp of Peri-Peri Seasoning
- 13/4 lbs. of sliced Pork Tenderloin

Instructions

- Preheat the oven to 425 degrees Fahrenheit. Mix tomatoes, oil, garlic, thyme, salt & pepper in a mixing bowl.
- Roast approximately 40 mins onto a baking sheet coated using parchment paper.
- To make steaks, cut the cauliflower lengthwise.
- Sprinkle cauliflower steaks using salt & pepper on a different lined baking sheet.
- Cook for about 30 minutes with cooking spray.
- Preheat the grill to high. Using peri-peri spice, coat pork medallions.
- Grill medallions about two minutes per side.
- Toss pork medallions using cauliflower steak & roasted tomatoes; however, if preferred, garnish over cilantro.

Nutrients: Calories: 300kcal, Carbs: 10g, Protein: 43g, Fat: 10g

35. Lean and Green Greek Yogurt with Pork Slaw

Prep Time: 10mins

Cook Time: 60mins

Servings: 4

Lean: 2

Green: 2

Condiments: 1

Ingredients

- 1 can Cooking Spray
- 1 1/2 lbs. of Pork Tenderloin
- 1 (12oz.) can of Diet Root Beer
- 3 cups shredded Red Cabbage
- 3 cups of shredded Green Cabbage
- 1/2 cup Greek Yogurt Non-Fat
- 2 tsp of Lemon Juice
- 1 tbsp of Apple Cider Vinegar
- 4 sachets of Cheddar Buttermilk Herb Biscuit
- 1 tsp of Dijon Mustard
- 1 Stevia
- 1/4 tsp of Celery Salt
- 1/2 cup of BBQ Sauce Sugar-Free

Instructions

- Spray the interior of the Instant Pot. Brown the pork slices on all sides, approximately 3 minutes on each side, on a hot sauté setting.
- Close the pressure valve, then add the diet root beer.
- Set the timer for 60 minutes on high.
- Wait for natural pressure to free before opening.
- Prepare the slaw in the meanwhile.
- Combine the following eight ingredients inside a mixing basin.
- Remove the pork from the Instant Pot and shred it in a basin.
- Toss in the barbecue sauce and mix well.
- Bake Cheddar Herb Buttermilk Biscuits as per the package instructions, if desired.
- Serve the pulled pork & slaw on top of biscuits or on their own.

Nutrients: Calories: 58kcal, Carbs: 11g, Protein: 4g, Fat: 1g

36. Spice-Rubbed Pork Chops Baked

Prep Time: 15mins

Cook Time: 15mins

Servings: 4

Lean: 1

Green: 1

Condiments: 3

Ingredients

- 1 teaspoon chili powder
- 1 Tablespoon of coconut sugar
- 1/2 teaspoon of cinnamon
- 1/4 teaspoon of onion powder
- 1/4 teaspoon of garlic powder
- Salt and pepper to taste
- 1/4 teaspoon of smoked paprika
- 1/2 teaspoon of sea salt
- Dried oregano
- 1/4 teaspoon of black pepper
- 2 carrots
- 2 parsnips
- 2–3 Tablespoons of olive oil
- Lemon slices & fresh herbs
- 1 1/2 pounds of pork chops boneless

Instructions

- In a dish, mix spice rub components and leave aside.
- Preheat oven to 400 °F and grease one baking sheet.
- Mix the parsnips & carrots with 2 olive oil and spice rub seasonings in a 1/2-inch baking dish.
- Roast parsnips & carrots for fifteen min, flattening them out on the lined baking sheet.
- Sprinkle every pork chop liberally with some spice rub while the vegetables are cooking.
- Place oil in every pork chop inside the pan.
- Caramelize them for 2 to 3 minutes over moderate heat, turning halfway through.
- Put pork chops onto a baking sheet with veggies after removing from heat.
- Return the baking sheet to oven for another 6-8 minutes.

- Take the baking sheet out from oven and, toss in some fresh parsley lemon slices, and season with salt & pepper to taste.

Nutrients: Calories: 247kcal, Carbs: 13g, Protein: 25g, Fat: 7g

37. Pork Chops Orange-Sage

Prep Time: 15mins

Cook Time: 15mins

Servings: 4

Lean: 2

Green: 1

Condiments: 2

Ingredients

- Salt and black pepper
- 4 pork chops boneless
- 3 Tbsp of I Can't Believe It's Not Butter Spread
- 1/4 cup of chicken broth low-sodium
- 1 1/4 tsp of cornstarch
- 2 tsp of sage leaves
- 1 tsp of orange zest
- 1 1/2 tsp of lemon juice
- 1/4 cup of orange juice
- 1 minced clove garlic
- 2 tsp of honey

Instructions

- Sprinkle pork chops with salt and ground pepper. In a pan, melt 2 tablespoons I Can't Believe It's Not Butter on moderate flame.
- Cook, flipping once, till pork chops have cooked through, approximately 4 minutes every side. Place on a platter, cover using foil and set aside for 3 minutes.
- Next, combine 1 tbsp. Broth and cornstarch in a mixing bowl.

- Combine the remaining 3 tablespoons broth, lemon juice, orange juice, and honey in a mixing bowl.
- Reduce pan temperature to moderate after extracting pork chops from the skillet.
- In the same skillet, melt the remaining 1 tablespoon I Can't Believe It's Not Butter.
- Sauté for 20 seconds or till garlic is gently browned.
- Re-whisk the mixture of orange juice, then spoon it in the pan, scraping the base to release any browned pieces.
- Boil the mixture, whisking continually, then lower to a low flame and let simmer for 1 minute, stirring often.
- Combine the orange zest & sage in a mixing bowl.
- Return the pork chops to the pan with the sauce spooned over them.
- Warm the dish before serving.

Nutrients: Calories: 182kcal, Carbs: 5g, Protein: 18g, Fat: 9g

38. Pork Loin Roasted with Apple Jus &Sweet Potato

Prep Time: 30mins

Cook Time: 60mins

Servings: 3

Lean: 2

Green: 0

Condiments: 2

Ingredients
- 3 tablespoons of canola oil
- 4 sweet potatoes
- ¼ teaspoon of cumin
- Pepper
- Salt
- 8 ounces of pork loin
- 5 cups of kale leaves

- 1 cup chicken stock low-sodium
- 5 chopped cloves garlic
- 1 chopped apple
- 1 tablespoon of honey

Instructions
- Preheat oven at 400 degrees Fahrenheit and prepare a baking tray.
- On a baking tray, mix sweet potatoes using 1 tbsp oil & cumin. Salt & pepper to taste.
- Using paper towels, pat the meat dry. Salt and black pepper to taste.
- 1 tbsp oil, heated in a pan over moderate heat. Sear the pork for 1-2 minutes on each side.
- Transfer meat to a baking tray and bake 20-25 minutes, saving pan juices.
- Allow 5 minutes for resting. Pork should be thinly sliced.
- Return the skillet to moderate flame, along with any remaining pan juices.
- Cook, stirring constantly, for approximately a minute till garlic is aromatic.
- Combine the honey, stock, and apple in a mixing bowl.
- Boil it, then lower to low heat and cook for 15-20 minutes.
- Heat the leftover 1 tbsp oil in a pan over moderate flame.
- Season greens with pepper and salt.
- Cook, stirring periodically, for approximately 5 minutes or until kale is tender.
- Drizzle the jus over the meat, sweet potatoes, and greens.
- Allow leftovers to cool fully before keeping them in the refrigerator in a sealed jar.

Nutrients: Calories: 506kcal, Carbs: 23g, Protein: 28g, Fat: 18g

39. Pork Souvlaki and Lemon Rice

Prep Time: 20mins

Cook Time: 40mins

Servings: 6

Lean: 1

Green: 0

Condiments: 2

Ingredients

- 3 Meyer lemons
- 2 pounds of pork tenderloin
- 1/2 cup of fruity olive oil
- 3 tablespoons of oregano
- 2 tablespoons of Italian parsley minced
- 6 minced garlic cloves
- 3 teaspoons of kosher salt
- 1 cup of white rice
- 1 teaspoon of fresh black pepper
- 1 tablespoon of Butter

Instructions

- Cut pork tenderloin in 1-inch slices after trimming the fat.
- Put a gallon bag of plastic in the freezer.
- Lemons should be zested and left ready for lemon rice.
- Mix olive oil and the juice of two Meyer lemons, saving one lemon to puree for lemon rice.
- Combine the garlic, kosher salt, oregano, & black pepper in a mixing bowl.
- Sprinkle over pork inside the plastic bag, close securely to exclude air, and refrigerate for at least 2 hours.
- Preheat a grill to moderate flame when you want to cook.
- Take the pork out from the marinade and throw it away.
- Metal skewers that were soaked for 20 minutes are used to attach the meat.
- When the grill is starting to heat up, combine 2 cups water, lemon zest, rice, Butter, saved lemon juice, and salt in a pan.
- Over high temperature, boil it, then lower to low heat and cover.

- Simmer for twenty minutes, then remove from the heat and set aside for 10 minutes to cool.
- Fuzz with fork, then season to taste using kosher salt & pepper, as well as 1 tablespoon chopped parsley.
- When the rice cooks, brown your pork on both sides, flipping every several minutes until it reaches 160 degrees F.
- Place on a serving tray, cover using foil and set aside for five min.
- Serve over lemon rice, garnished with parsley as well as a lemon if desired.

Nutrients: Calories: 312kcal, Carbs: 20g, Protein: 26g, Fat: 13g

40. Bake Pork and Pan Shake Chops

Prep Time: 15mins

Cook Time: 25mins

Servings: 4

Lean: 1

Green: 2

Condiments: 3

Ingredients:

- Kosher salt & ground black pepper
- 4 pork chops
- 2 eggs
- 1 and a half cups of Panko
- 1/4 cup of milk
- Half tsp garlic powder
- 1/4 tsp of dried oregano
- Quarter tsp of onion powder
- 1/4 teaspoon of dried basil
- 1/4 teaspoon of dried parsley
- Kosher salt & black pepper
- 1/4 teaspoon of dried thyme
- Quarter teaspoon of smoked paprika
- 1 pound of brussels sprouts

- 1/4 cup of vegetable oil
- One Gala apple
- 2 tablespoons of brown sugar
- 3 tablespoons of olive oil
- 1/4 teaspoon of dried sage
- 1 teaspoon of dried rosemary

Instructions

- Preheat oven at 425 degrees Fahrenheit.
- Spray a baking pan with nonstick cooking spray.
- Combine the brussels sprouts, olive oil, apple, rosemary, brown sugar, and sage in a mixing bowl; sprinkle with pepper and salt.
- Sprinkle pork chops with pepper and salt.
- Mix together milk and eggs in a mixing dish.
- Combine garlic powder, Panko, oregano, basil, onion powder, thyme, paprika, parsley, & vegetable oil inside a separate mixing bowl; sprinkle to taste using pepper and salt.
- Dip pork chops inside the egg mixture one by one time, and dip in Panko mixture, compressing to coat.
- Put the pork chops on the lined baking sheet and surround them with the mixture of brussels sprouts.
- Preheat oven to 350°F and cook for 10 to 12 minutes.
- Cook for a further 10-12 minutes.

Nutrients: Calories: 757kcal, Carbs: 39g, Protein: 46g, Fat: 47g

41. Tofu Bowl Lean and Green

Prep Time: 9mins

Cook Time: 21mins

Servings: 1

Lean: 2

Green: 1

Condiments: 2

Ingredients

- 1 tsp. of Sesame Oil
- 15 oz of Firm Tofu
- 1 tsp. of Rice Vinegar
- Half cup of eggplant cubed
- Half cup of kale chopped
- Half cup of cauliflower grated
- 2 tbsp. of Soy Sauce Low Sodium

Instructions

- Tofu should be pressed.
- Put tofu slices on a plate or chopping board and cover with many layers of towels.
- On the tofu, add a layer of towel. On top of the second layer, put a weight.
- Allow tofu to settle for 15 minutes before cutting into 1-inch pieces.
- In a skillet, heat the sesame oil. On the opposite side, arrange the cubed eggplant.
- Cook for 10-12 minutes. Remove the pan from the heat and put it aside.
- Sauté the soy sauce, kale, & rice vinegar till the kale is wilted.
- In a microwave-safe dish, heat grated cauliflower for approximately 3-4 minutes.
- In the bowl, combine cauliflower rice, eggplant, tofu, and kale.

Nutrients: Calories: 412kcal, Carbs: 6g, Protein:50 g, Fat:26 g

42. Lean and Green Zucchini Pappardelle with Mushroom and Tofu Stroganoff

Prep Time: 10mins

Cook Time: 20mins

Servings: 4

Lean: 0

Green: 4

Condiments: 1-2

Ingredients

- 10 oz. of Yellow Squash
- 10 oz. of Zucchini
- 2 minced Garlic Cloves
- 3 1/2 lbs. of sliced tofu Extra Firm
- 1/4 tsp of Black Pepper
- 3 stalks of Scallions diced
- 1 1/2 cups of Vegetable Stock
- 1 stalk of Fresh Thyme
- 1 tbsp Soy Sauce Low Sodium
- 8 oz sliced Cremini mushrooms
- 1/4 tsp of Salt
- 1/4 cup of Sour Cream

Instructions

- Use a vegetable peeler, spiralizer, or mandolin, or shave zucchini or yellow squash in broad noodles.
- In a pan, combine the scallions, garlic, tofu, veggie stock, stock, thyme, soy sauce, and mushrooms.
- Boil for 5-8 minutes. While they are cooking, bring a saucepan to a simmer, then blanch the zucchini and yellow squash for 2-5 minutes.
- Drain thoroughly. Stir inside the sour cream after removing the tofu mix from heat.
- If desired, sprinkle pepper and salt. Serve stroganoff over pappardelle made from zucchini or yellow squash.

Nutrients: Calories: 356kcal, Carbs:42 g, Protein:21 g, Fat:12 g

43. Bean Lasagna Lean and Green

Prep Time: 5mins

Cook Time: 20mins

Servings: 1

Lean: 3

Green: 1

Condiments: 1

Ingredients

- 1/4 tsp. of Garlic Salt
- 1.5 cups of Green Beans
- 1/2 tsp. of Basil
- 1 tbsp. of Parmesan Cheese Reduced Fat
- 1/4 cup of Ricotta Cheese, Part Skim
- 3/4 cup of Mozzarella Cheese Reduced Fat
- 2 tbsp. of Rao's Marinara Sauce

Instructions

- Green beans should be prepared and placed inside a baking tray.
- Combine the garlic salt, ricotta cheese, and basil in a mixing bowl.
- Pour the sauce over the green beans. On ricotta cheese mix, pour marinara sauce.
- Top with a sprinkling of mozzarella cheese.
- Bake for twenty minutes at 350 degrees Fahrenheit, then broil till cheese is gently browned.
- Parmesan cheese should be sprinkled on top.

Nutrients: Calories: 328kcal, Carbs:39 g, Protein:23 g, Fat:9 g

44. Bean Casserole Lean and Green

Prep Time: 10mins

Cook Time: 35mins

Servings: 4

Lean: 3

Green: 2

Condiments: 1

Ingredients

- 3-dash Cooking Spray

- 1-16 oz. of Green Beans
- 2 cups chopped Button Mushrooms
- 1 small minced Garlic Cloves
- 2 tbsp. of grated Parmesan Cheese
- 1/4 cup diced Yellow Onion
- 3/4 cup Greek yogurt non-Fat
- 1 tsp. of Cornstarch
- 1/4 cup of Sour Cream
- 1/2 packet of Stevia
- 1/2 tsp. of Black Pepper
- 1/2 tsp. of Salt
- 1/2 cup of shredded cheddar Cheese Reduced-Fat

Instructions

- Preheat oven to 350 degrees Fahrenheit.
- Green beans should be microwaved as per package recommendations.
- Heat a pan on moderate heat, lightly greased. Cook for 5-7 minutes.
- In a mixing dish, combine the mushroom combination with the green beans, then set aside to chill.
- In a mixing bowl, add Greek yogurt, cornstarch, sour cream, salt, stevia, and pepper.
- Toss the veggies in the sauce until they are equally covered. Mix in the cheddar cheese till everything is nicely mixed.
- Spread it into a lightly oiled baking dish, cover with Parmesan, then bake for 30-35 minutes.

Nutrients: Calories:223 kcal, Carbs:26 g, Protein:12 g, Fat:8 g

45. Calabacitas

Prep Time: 5mins

Cook Time: 20mins

Servings: 6

Lean: 1

Green: 2

Condiments: 2

Ingredients

- 1 diced onion
- 1 tbsp. of olive oil
- 1 diced poblano pepper
- 1 15-ounce can of drained kernel corn
- 1 diced jalapeno pepper
- 2 diced plum tomatoes
- 1 yellow squash
- 1 zucchini
- 3 minced cloves garlic
- 1/4 tsp. of black pepper
- 2 tsp. of kosher salt
- 1/4 tsp. of dried oregano
- 1/4 cup of water
- 1/4 tsp. of ground cumin
- Chopped cilantro
- 1/2 cup of cheddar cheese shredded
- Cotija cheese crumbled
- 1/4 cup of milk

Instructions

- In a nonstick skillet, heat the olive oil on moderate heat.
- Combine the poblanos, onions, and jalapenos in a mixing bowl.
- Cook, stirring regularly, about 5 minutes.
- Toss in the corn & tomatoes. Cook for another 5 minutes, stirring once in a while.
- Combine the zucchini, garlic, yellow squash, salt, oregano, black pepper, & ground cumin in a mixing bowl.
- Cook about five min, turning each minute.
- In a pan, add water, decrease heat to low, then cover, and cook for 5 mins.
- Uncover the pan and whisk in the milk and cheese until the cheese is completely melted.
- Remove from the heat and serve with cilantro & cotija cheese.

Nutrients: Calories: 40kcal, Carbs:4 g, Protein:1 g, Fat: 2g

46. Garlic Zoodles, Roasted

Prep Time: 5mins

Cook Time: 10mins

Servings: 1

Lean: 1

Green: 1

Condiments: 1

Ingredients

- Chopped parsley
- 3/4 tbsp. of olive oil
- 1 zucchini
- 2 Minced garlic cloves
- 1/4 tsp. of dried parsley
- 1/4 tsp. of paprika
- 2 tbsp. of grated Parmesan
- Salt & pepper

Instructions

- Preheat the oven to 400 degrees Fahrenheit. Using foil, prepare a baking pan.
- Zucchini should be spiralized.
- Mix zucchini, paprika, garlic, dried parsley, pepper, salt, & olive oil inside a mixing bowl.
- On your baking tray, spread evenly.
- Preheat oven to 400°F and bake for ten min.
- Stir with Parmesan cheese just after taking it out from the oven.
- Chopped parsley may be used as a garnish.

Nutrients: Calories:146 kcal, Carbs:3 g, Protein:5 g, Fat: 13g

47. Carrot Spaghetti with Mushroom Bolognese

Prep Time: 15mins

Cook Time: 45mins

Servings: 4

Lean: 0

Green: 2

Condiments: 2

Ingredients

- 1tsp Olive oil
- 20 g Mushrooms
- 1 chopped Brown onion
- ½ tsp Stock powder, gluten-free and vegetable variety
- 500 g Mushrooms
- 1 Chopped Celery
- 2 crushed Garlic cloves
- 400 g Canned tomatoes
- 2 tsp Balsamic vinegar
- 2 cups Tomato passata
- 500 g Carrot
- ½ cups basil

Instructions

- In a heatproof bowl, put the porcini mushrooms.
- Set it aside about 10 minutes after covering using one cup boiling water.
- Using a strainer, strain porcini water in a basin, removing the mushrooms.
- Next, in a nonstick pan, heat the oil on medium-high heat.
- Cook onion & celery for five min, stirring occasionally.
- Cook, stirring occasionally, for another 5 minutes after adding mushrooms & garlic.
- Combine the vinegar, passata, porcini water, tomatoes, and basil in a mixing bowl.
- Boil it, season with pepper and salt. Reduce heat to low and cook, covered, for thirty min.
- On moderate flame, heat a frying pan.
- Cook, whisking, for five min, adding stock powder, carrot, and water.
- Lower the heat, then whisk in half of the Bolognese sauce.

- Divide the carrot spaghetti among four bowls, then top with the leftover Bolognese sauce.
- Add more basil leaves if desired.

Nutrients: Calories:548 kcal, Carbs:80 g, Protein:16 g, Fat:16 g

48. Loaded Vegetable Stir-Fry

Prep Time: 20mins

Cook Time: 10mins

Servings: 4

Lean: 0

Green: 4

Condiments: 2

Ingredients

- 1 Carrot
- 1 Brown onion sliced
- 1 thinly sliced Red capsicum
- 2 crushed Garlic cloves
- 100 g sliced Shiitake mushrooms
- 1 chopped Red chili
- Oil spray
- 200 g trimmed Snow peas
- 1 tbsp Fresh ginger
- ½ tsp Stock powder
- Chinese cabbage shredded 250 g,
- 1 tbs Kecapmanis
- ¼ cup Fresh coriander
- Zucchini 600 g, spiralized
- 1 tbsp Lime juice

Instructions

- Heat a big frying pan on high heat, lightly spray with oil.
- 5 mins of stir-frying onion, capsicum, carrot, and mushrooms.
- Stir in the chili, garlic, snow peas, ginger, and cabbage for another minute.

- With a small pitcher, mix stock powder into 1 tbsp hot water.
- Stir-fry for about two min, adding kecapmanis, stock, and zucchini to the pan.
- Toss in the coriander & lime juice to mix. Serve using lime wedges & additional sliced chili.

Nutrients: Calories: 30kcal, Carbs:5 g, Protein:1 g, Fat: 0g

49. Turkey Salad with Beetroot Patties

Prep Time: 15mins

Cook Time: 15mins

Servings: 4

Lean: 1

Green: 3

Condiments: 2

Ingredients

- 500 g Turkey breast mince
- Cooked beetroot grated 250 g
- 2 Chopped Green shallots
- 1 Egg
- 1 crushed Garlic clove
- Oil spray
- ½ cup chopped flat-leaf parsley
- 200g Tomato
- 2 tsp grated lemon rind
- 1 sliced Lebanese cucumber

- 2 tsp Balsamic vinegar
- 4 cups of Rockets

Instructions

- To drain extra liquid, place beetroot onto a tea towel, bring ends together, twist, then squeeze.
- Place the beets in a large mixing basin.
- Combine the mince, garlic, shallots, egg, rind and parsley in a mixing bowl.
- Mix in the pepper and salt.
- Divide the mixture in 12 parts using moist hands.
- Make patties. Refrigerate while preparing the salad on a baking tray.
- In a serving dish, combine tomatoes, rockets, cucumber, and vinegar.
- Toss to incorporate and add salt & pepper.
- Heat a big frying pan on moderate heat, lightly sprayed with oil.
- Heat patties for 3 to 4 minutes on every side in batches.
- Garnish patties with shallots & salad.

Nutrients: Calories:183 kcal, Carbs:7 g, Protein:30 g, Fat: 4g

50. Chicken Traybake and Cauliflower Rice

Prep Time: 10mins
Cook Time: 10 hrs. 30mins
Servings: 4
Lean: 1
Green: 5
Condiments: 1

Ingredients

- ⅓ cup Teriyaki sauce
- 450 g chicken breast skinless
- 2 tbsp Sesame oil
- 180 g Sugar snap peas
- 3 sliced Green shallot
- 300 g Broccoli
- 1 Carrot
- 1 Cauliflower
- 1 Red capsicum

Instructions

- In a mixing dish, mix 2 tbsp teriyaki sauce, chicken strips, and 1 tsp sesame oil.
- While the oven is heating, cover and leaves away in the refrigerator to marinate.
- Place a big baking pan in the oven with foil-lined sides.
- Preheat the oven to 200 degrees Celsius.
- In a bowl, toss the broccoli, carrot, snap peas, capsicum, and leftover sesame oil to cover thoroughly.
- Remove the pan from the oven.
- Spread the chicken & vegetable mixture on the tray's base.
- Bake for twenty minutes.
- Meanwhile, inside a food processor, pulse cauliflower until it resembles rice.
- Take the tray out of the oven. Stir your cauliflower 'rice' into the tray carefully to mix it.
- Cook for an additional 8 to 10 minutes.
- Remove the baking pan from the oven. Preheat the grill in the oven to moderate.
- Over the chicken and veggies on the tray, drizzle the leftover teriyaki sauce. Grill for two to three minutes.
- Serve with shallots on top.

Nutrients: Calories:656 kcal, Carbs:9 g, Protein: 41g, Fat: 49g

Chapter no. 5 Dinner Recipes

1. Chicken Zoodle Lean and Green Alfredo

Prep Time: 10mins

Cook Time: 15mins

Servings: 4

Lean: 3

Green: 1

Condiments: 1

Ingredients
- 2 tsp of Olive Oil, Extra Virgin
- 2 cups of Riced Cauliflower Frozen
- 3/4 cup of Parmesan Cheese Reduced-Fat
- 2 pinches of Fresh Parsley
- 1/2 tsp of Salt
- 1 half lbs. of Chicken Breast
- 2 Scallions
- 4 cups of Zucchini Noodles
- 2 Cheese Wedge Laughing Cow

Instructions
- Cook cauliflower in an oven for 4 mins till soft.
- In a mixer, blend the prepared cauliflower and salt, cheese wedges, parmesan, scallion, and water until smooth.
- Remove and keep warm. In a hot pan, cook the zucchini noodles for two minutes with olive oil.
- Combine the chicken and sauce of cauliflower alfredo.
- Divide the mixture into 4 equal parts and top with 1 tbsp of parmesan cheese.
- If necessary, garnish using parsley.

Nutrients Calories: 315kcal, Carbs: 13g, Protein: 16g, Fat: 22g

2. Chicken Burritos Lean and Green

Prep Time: 15mins

Cook Time: 24mins

Servings: 8

Lean: 3

Green: 2

Condiments: 2-3

Ingredients
- 1/2 cup of Egg Beaters
- 2 cups of cauliflower grated
- 1/4 tsp of Black Pepper
- 3 oz of Chicken Breast Cooked
- 2 tbsp of Cilantro
- 1/8 tsp of Salt
- 1 half oz of Avocado
- 1 oz shredded Mexican Cheese Low Fat

Instructions
- Preheat the oven. Using parchment paper, line a sheet pan.
- Microwave cauliflower for 2 minutes, stirring halfway through, then cook for another 2 minutes, stirring halfway through.
- Remove any extra water by squeezing it out.
- Combine the cauliflower, pepper, eggs, and salt in a large mixing basin.
- Make 6 rounds out of the mixture on baking sheet.

- Bake for 10 minutes, then turn and bake for another 5-7 minutes.
- Allow it to cool. Combine the chicken, cheese, avocado, and Cilantro in a mixing bowl.
- Fill every cauliflower tortilla with 1/4 of the filling and roll it up.
- Using frying spray, coat a pan or griddle.
- Heat burritos for 2 minutes over medium heat, flip, and cook for 1 minute more or till golden.

Nutrients Calories: 260kcal, Carbs: 116g, Protein: 50g, Fat: 29g

3. Green cheesy Bacon Keto and Low-Carb Lean Smothered Chicken

Prep Time: 10mins

Cook Time: 25mins

Servings: 3

Lean: 3

Green: 2

Condiments: 2

Ingredients

- 3 tsp of Olive Oil
- 10 oz of sliced Chicken Breast Cooked
- 6 slices of chopped Bacon
- 1 cup of Vanilla Almond Milk Unsweetened
- 4 slices of Mozzarella Cheese Low Fat
- 1/4 tsp of Salt
- 1 slice chopped Tomatoes Sun Dried
- 1/2 cup of Chicken Broth
- 1/2 tsp of Black Pepper
- 1 tsp of Garlic Powder
- 5 tbsp of grated Parmesan Cheese Reduced-Fat
- 1 tsp of Parsley
- 1 cup of chopped spinach

Instructions

- Cook Canadian bacon, then remove it and remove the grease.
- Slice the bacon. Keep it aside. Add some olive oil to the skillet.
- Cook the thin slices of chicken in a pan over medium heat for 4 mins.
- Add the chicken broth, almond milk, parsley, garlic powder, salt, parmesan cheese and pepper to the skillet.
- Whisk constantly until it thickens.
- Allow boiling until spinach begins to wilt, then add spinach tomatoes.
- Add the pieces of chicken one by one. Lightly cover each chicken piece with sauce, then top using mozzarella cheese and crumbled bacon. Cover for 1 min.

Nutrients Calories: 596kcal, Carbs: 4g, Protein: 69g, Fat: 38g

4. Pot Chicken Lean and Green Cacciatore

Prep Time: 15mins

Cook Time: 30mins

Servings: 4

Lean: 1

Green: 3-4

Condiments: 1

Ingredients

- 1/4 tsp of Salt
- 2 lbs. of Skinless Boneless Chicken Thighs
- 1/2 tsp of Black Pepper
- 1 cup of Crushed Tomatoes
- 1 can of Cooking spray
- 2 tbsp of Fresh Parsley
- 1/2 cup of Scallions
- 1/4 cup of Bell Peppers Green
- 1/2 cup of Bell Peppers Red
- 1 Bay Leaf

- 1/2 tsp of Dried Onion

Instructions

- On all sides, season the chicken using pepper and salt.
- In Instant Pot, press sauté, gently spray cooking oil, then brown all sides for 2-3 minutes.
- Add onions & peppers after spraying with some extra oil.
- Sauté for five min or until softened and browned.
- Spoon the tomatoes on the chicken & veggies, toss in the salt, bay leaf, and pepper, then over.
- Cook on high pressure for about 25 minutes, then release naturally.
- Remove the bay leaf, sprinkle with parsley, then serve on your third green of choice.

Nutrients Calories: 310kcal, Carbs: 15g, Protein: 38g, Fat: 12g

5. Lean and Green Grilled Marinated Chicken Root Beer

Prep Time: 10mins

Cook Time: 180mins

Servings: 3

Lean: 1

Green: 0

Condiments: 1

Ingredients

- 2 tbsp of Apple Cider Vinegar
- 1.5 lbs. of Skinless Boneless Chicken Breast
- 12oz. can of Root Beer, Diet
- 1/2 cup of Soy Sauce Low Sodium
- 2 tbsp of Vegetable Oil

Instructions

- In a mixing bowl, combine vinegar, root beer, soy sauce and vegetable oil.
- Add chicken and let it sit and marinate for 3 hours.
- Preheat the grill to high heat. To avoid sticking, spray with veggie spray.
- Grill until the chicken reaches an internal temperature of 165°F.

Nutrients Calories: 4219kcal, Carbs: 424g, Protein: 320g, Fat: 140g

6. Lean and Green Chicken Chili

Prep Time: 10mins

Cook Time: 35mins

Servings: 4

Lean: 3

Green: 1

Condiments: 2

Ingredients

- 1 tbsp of Olive Oil
- 2 1/4 lbs. of Skinless, Boneless chopped Chicken Breast
- 1 cup of diced Green Onions
- 1/4 cup of diced Jalapeño Pepper
- 1 cup of chopped Red Bell Peppers
- 3 minced Garlic Cloves
- 2 tsp of Cumin
- 1 Cilantro
- 1/2 tsp of Salt
- 1 tsp of Coriander
- 1 cup of Water
- 3 cups of Chicken Broth
- 3 tbsp of Coconut Milk Unsweetened
- 2 (7) oz of Green Chilies

Instructions

- Cut the chicken and vegetables. Then, on medium heat, set a big saucepan.

- Combine the onions, oil, peppers, jalapeno, and garlic in a large mixing bowl.
- Cook for five min over medium-high heat.
- Combine the chicken, salt, and spices in a mixing bowl.
- Cook for another 5 - 10 minutes.
- Combine the green chilies, broth, & coconut milk. Bring the water to a boil.
- Reduce the heat to low and cook for twenty minutes.

Nutrients Calories: 109kcal, Carbs: 21g, Protein: 21g, Fat: 12g

7. Chicken Stuffed Lean and Green Broccoli and Cheese

Prep Time: 10mins

Cook Time: 26mins

Servings: 4

Lean: 2

Green: 1

Condiments: 2

Ingredients
- 1/4 tsp of Salt
- 4 (6) oz of Skinless Boneless Chicken Breast
- 1/4 tsp of Black Pepper
- 1 tsp of Onion Powder
- 1 tsp of Garlic Powder
- 1/4 tsp of Paprika
- 1 tbsp of Olive Oil
- 1 cup finely chopped Red Bell Peppers
- 1 cup finely chopped broccoli floret
- 1 tbsp of Light Mayonnaise
- 1 cup of Cheddar Cheese Low Fat

Instructions
- Preheat the oven at 425 degrees Fahrenheit.
- Combine the salt, garlic, pepper, onion, & paprika in a mixing bowl.

- Split the mixture in two and sprinkle both sides of the chicken breasts.
- Make a pocket for broccoli & cheese filling by cutting a slice through the center of the roast chicken.
- Microwave broccoli with 2 tbsp of water in a microwave-safe dish.
- Microwave for one minute, covered. Remove any excess water.
- Place the cheese, bell pepper, mayonnaise, and the leftover spice combination between chicken breasts in the dish.
- The stuffing of the chicken breast is frequently secured with a toothpick.
- 1 tbsp oil, heated in a cast iron pan over moderate flame.
- On every side, cook the chicken for about 3 minutes.
- After searing, place the pan with foil & bake for 15-17 mins, or till the internal temperature of the chicken reaches 165°F.
- Set aside about 5 minutes.

Nutrients Calories: 300kcal, Carbs: 22g, Protein: 17g, Fat: 16g

8. Chicken and Paella with Soy Chorizo Lean and Green

Prep Time: 10mins

Cook Time: 17mins

Servings: 4

Lean: 2

Green: 3

Condiments: 2

Ingredients

- 2 oz of Seitan Chorizo Crumbles
- 4 tsp of Canola Oil
- 1 half lbs. Skinless Boneless Chicken Breast
- 1 stalk of Scallions minced
- 2 minced Garlic Cloves
- 4 cups of Riced Cauliflower
- 1 tsp of Salt
- 1 cup of Green Beans
- 1 cup of Diced Tomatoes
- 1/4 tsp of Black Pepper

Instructions

- Cook the crumbles of soy chorizo and chicken in a big pan with canola oil on high until golden but not entirely cooked.
- Sweat the scallions and minced garlic for about two min with the cover on.
- Toss the paella with tomatoes, cauliflower rice, & green beans.
- Cook for about ten min. Add salt & pepper and serve immediately.

Nutrients Calories: 563kcal, Carbs: 62g, Protein: 38g, Fat: 16g

9. Lemon Chicken Lean and Green Spaghetti Squash and Spinach with Tomatoes

Prep Time: 13mins

Cook Time: 32mins

Servings: 4

Lean: 2

Green: 4

Condiments: 3

Ingredients

- 1/2 tsp of salt divided
- 2 lbs. of Skinless Boneless Chicken Breast
- 1/2 tsp of Black Pepper
- 1/4 cup of Yellow Onion
- 1 tbsp of Olive Oil
- 2 minced Garlic Cloves
- 2 cups of Baby Spinach
- 4 cups of Spaghetti Squash
- 1 cup of Cherry Tomatoes
- 1/2 Lemons
- 1 cup Chicken Broth Low Sodium

Instructions

- Season the chicken breasts with salt and pepper.
- In a pan, heat the olive oil on medium heat.
- Cook for 7 to 10 minutes or until chicken is cooked through.
- Take the chicken out of the pan and put it aside.
- In a pan, sauté the onion and garlic until aromatic, approximately 1-2 minutes.
- Cook, stirring occasionally, until tomatoes start to soften, about two to three minutes.
- Reduce the heat to low, add chicken broth, salt and lemon juice, and simmer until the water has reduced to half, about 15 minutes.
- Cook, stirring occasionally, until the spinach has wilted, about 2 minutes.
- On the spaghetti squash, spoon the ingredients of the skillet.

Nutrients Calories: 489kcal, Carbs: 40g, Protein: 28g, Fat: 24g

10. Chicken Parmesan Lean and Green

Prep Time: 10mins

Cook Time: 20mins

Servings: 4

Lean: 1

Green: 2

Condiments: 1

Ingredients

- 1.75 lbs. of Skinless Boneless Chicken Breast
- 1/2 cup of Almond Flour
- 2 tbsp of Nutritional Yeast Large Flake
- 2 tsp of Nutritional Yeast Large Flake
- 1/2 tsp of salt divided
- 1/2 tsp of Black Pepper
- 1 (15oz.) tin of Diced Petite Tomatoes
- 1/2 tsp of Dried Oregano
- 2 minced Garlic Cloves
- 2 stalks of Scallions chopped
- 2 Zucchini spiraled

Instructions

- Preheat the oven to 400 degrees Fahrenheit.
- In a mixing bowl, mix the almond flour & flake nutritional yeast.
- Sprinkle the chicken breasts with pepper and salt before coating both surfaces with the mixture almond.
- Preheat the oven to 350°F and bake the chicken for 12-15 minutes, or till the inner temperature rises to 165°F.
- Take the chicken out from the oven after it's done cooking and lay it aside.
- Mix tomatoes, garlic, oregano, and scallions in a saucepan and cook on low for 15-20 minutes whilst chicken bakes.
- Chop and slice the zucchini. In a crockpot over hot water on the stovetop, cook zucchini noodles till soft.
- With marinara & chicken, offer zucchini noodles.

Nutrients Calories: 361kcal, Carbs: 26g, Protein: 32g, Fat: 10g

11. Mason Jar Lean and Green Chicken Parm Soup

Prep Time: 5mins

Cook Time: 5mins

Servings: 1

Lean: 2

Green: 1

Condiments: 0

Ingredients

- 2 tbsp Italian Salad Dressing Reduced-Fat
- 1/4 cup of tomato sauce No-sugar-added
- 1 Zucchini spiraled
- 8 oz Hot Water
- 2 tbsp of grated Parmesan Cheese
- 6 oz chopped Chicken Breast Cooked
- 1 tbsp of basil chopped

Instructions

- Fill the mason jar halfway with tomato sauce & Italian Dressing.
- Cooked chicken breast, parmesan, as well as basil are layered on top of zucchini noodles.
- To serve, fill a mason jar halfway with boiling water, then cover and set aside for five min.

Nutrients Calories: 323kcal, Carbs: 17g, Protein: 28g, Fat: 12g

12. Crock-Pot Lean and Green Chicken Taco

Prep Time: 10mins

Cook Time: 240mins

Servings: 2

Lean: 3

Green: 2

Condiments: 1

Ingredients

- 2 cups of Water
- 2 cups of Chicken Broth Low Sodium
- 1 cup of Diced Tomato and green chilies
- 1/2 tsp of Cumin
- 2 oz Mexican Cheese Blend, Reduced-Fat
- 1 tsp Taco Seasoning Mix Reduced Sodium
- 1/4 tsp of Chili Powder
- 13-14 oz Skinless Boneless Chicken Breast
- 1 minced Garlic Cloves
- 2 cups of chopped Green Cabbage

Instructions

- In crockpot, mix together the water, chicken broth, chopped tomatoes, cumin, taco seasoning, chili powder, cabbage, garlic, and chicken.
- Cook for 6-8 hours. Before eating, separate the chicken breast inside the crockpot.
- To serve, ladle soup in bowls and sprinkle with cheese.

Nutrients Calories: 200kcal, Carbs: 5g, Protein: 26g, Fat: 7g

13. Chicken Paella Lean and Green

Prep Time: 15mins

Cook Time: 15mins

Servings: 4

Lean: 2

Green: 3

Condiments: 2

Ingredients

- 2 oz Crumbles Seitan Chorizo
- 4 tsp of Canola Oil
- 11/2 lbs. Skinless Boneless diced Chicken Breast
- 1 stalk of Scallions minced
- 1/4 tsp of Black Pepper
- 2 Garlic Cloves
- 4 cups of Riced Cauliflower Frozen
- 1 cup of Diced Tomatoes
- 1 pinch of Saffron
- 1/4 tsp of Salt
- 1 cup of finely chopped Green Beans

Instructions

- Cook the crumbles of seitan chorizo & chicken in a pan over medium heat.
- Sweat for approximately 2 minutes with the garlic & onions.
- Toss the paella with the saffron, cauliflower rice, tomatoes & green beans.
- Cook for 10 min, season with pepper and salt and serve immediately.

Nutrients Calories: 380kcal, Carbs: 57g, Protein: 24g, Fat: 5g

14. Lean and Green Chicken Medley

Prep Time: 30mins

Cook Time: 20mins

Servings: 4

Lean: 1

Green: 1

Condiments: 2

Ingredients

- 3 cups of chopped Broccoli
- 2 lbs. of Skinless, Boneless sliced Chicken Breast
- 11/2 cup of chopped Red Bell Peppers

- 1/2 cup of Light Dressing of Lime Vinaigrette
- 1 can Cooking Spray
- 11/2 cup of chopped Yellow Bell Pepper
- 2 tsp of Onion Powder
- 1/2 oz of Pine Nuts
- 1 tsp of Blend of Garlic & Herb Seasoning

Instructions

- Using salad dressing, coat the chicken breasts.
- Season the chicken strips with the seasoning mix and onion powder.
- Allow 30 minutes for the strips to marinade.
- While the chicken is marinating, cook the peppers & broccoli till al dente in a sauté pan.
- When heating peppers, add water often so they don't burn.
- Remove the peppers & broccoli from the pan and set them aside.
- Cook the chicken in pan until it is not pink.
- In the meanwhile, roast pine nuts until golden brown.
- When the chicken is finished, toss in the peppers, pine nuts and broccoli, and serve right away.

Nutrients Calories: 279kcal, Carbs: 16.0g, Protein: 35.5g, Fat: 8.1g

15. Minestrone Soup Lean and Green

Prep Time: 15mins

Cook Time: 60mins

Servings: 4

Lean: 3

Green: 5

Condiments: 3

Ingredients

- 4 cups of Chicken Stock
- 11/4 lbs. Chicken Thigh Skinless
- 1 tsp of Salt
- 2 cups of shredded Green Cabbage
- 4 tsp Parmesan Cheese Low-fat
- 1 cup of celery sliced
- 1 cup of diced Yellow Squash
- 1 cup of Cherry Tomatoes
- 1 cup of Cauliflower Florets
- 1/4 tsp of Black Pepper
- 1 cup of Fresh Basil

Instructions

- In a pot, mix the chicken & stock and boil.
- Lower the heat and gently simmer for 45mins, or until the meat is cooked.
- Set the thighs of chicken aside to cool after removing them from broth.
- Add vegetables to broth and cook for another 10 minutes on low heat.
- When the chicken is cool enough to handle, shred it into bite-sized pieces.
- Return the chicken into the pot.
- Combine the basil, tomatoes, and pepper in a mixing bowl. Serve it.

Nutrients Calories: 203kcal, Carbs: 41g, Protein: 9g, Fat: 1g

16. Lean and Green Chicken and Cauliflower Asparagus Risotto

Prep Time: 10mins

Cook Time: 30mins

Servings: 4

Lean: 2

Green: 1

Condiments: 2

Ingredients

- 1/4 tsp of Salt
- 4 tbsp of Nutritional Yeast Large Flake
- 2 lbs. Skinless Boneless Chicken Breast
- 1/4 tsp of Black Pepper
- 11/4 lbs. of Riced Cauliflower
- 2 tbsp of Unsalted Butter
- 1/2 cup of Chicken Stock
- 1/4 lb. of chopped Asparagus

Instructions

- Preheat the oven to 350 degrees Fahrenheit.
- Season the chicken inside a casserole dish using salt and pepper.
- Spread melted butter over the chicken, then roast for 30 minutes.
- Remove from the oven and set aside to cool.
- In a separate saucepan, mix Asparagus, cauliflower rice, and chicken stock, then cook until cooked. Add the water as required.
- Once the risotto with cauliflower & Asparagus is done, take it out from the heat and stir in some nutritional yeast.
- Serve the risotto alongside roasted vegetables.

Nutrients Calories: 320kcal, Carbs: 13g, Protein: 43g, Fat: 11g

17. Pesto Lean and Green Zucchini Noodles and Grilled Chicken

Prep Time: 10mins

Cook Time: 15mins

Servings: 4

Lean: 2

Green: 2

Condiments:1

Ingredients

- 1/2 cup of basil chopped
- 1/3 cup of Italian Dressing Low Calorie
- 1/2 cup of Parmesan Cheese
- 1/2 tsp of Red Pepper Flakes Crushed
- 1 pt. of Cooking spray
- 1/3 oz of Pine Nuts
- 2 Zucchini
- 2 cups of Cherry Tomatoes
- 1 1/2 lbs. of Skinless Boneless Chicken Breast

Instructions

- To prepare the pesto in a stick blender, mix the salad, basil, Parmesan cheese, & pine nuts.
- Blend until completely smooth.
- Heat zucchini noodles in a lightly oiled pan over moderate heat until barely soft, approximately 3-5 minutes.
- Remove from the heat inside the pesto & leftover Parmesan cheese.
- Toss in the tomatoes, then top using grilled chicken & red pepper flakes.

Nutrients Calories: 480kcal, Carbs: 18g, Protein: 40g, Fat: 30g

18. Lean and Green Turkey Meatloaf and Fennel

Prep Time: 8mins

Cook Time: 37mins

Servings: 4

Lean: 3

Green: 3

Condiments: 1-2

Ingredients

- 3 cups of Napa Cabbage
- 2 lbs. of Lean Turkey Ground
- 2 stalks of minced Green Onions
- 1 tsp of Paprika

- 1/4 cup of crushed Pine Nuts
- 1 tsp of Salt
- 1 tbsp of Olive Oil
- 2 tbsp of Parmesan Cheese
- 1 tsp of Black Pepper
- 2/3 cup of Chicken Stock
- 2 Fennel Bulbs

Instructions

- Preheat the oven at 350 degrees Fahrenheit.
- In the oven, pine nuts for approximately 5-7 minutes.
- Following roasting pine nuts, preheat oven to 400°F.
- Mix the Napa cabbage, ground turkey, green onions, paprika, pine nuts, salt and black pepper in a mixing bowl.
- Place the turkey mixture on the sheet pan and arrange it into a meatloaf that is 7 inches in length and 4 inches broad.
- Cook the loaf for approximately 30mins, or until it reaches a temp of 165°F on the inside.
- Cut the green stems from the fennel, then cut the bulb in half while the loaf is baking.
- Remove the central core from every fennel half, then cut it into quarter wedges.
- A few of the beautiful fronds should be saved and roughly trimmed for subsequent use.
- Cook fennel wedges in a nonstick pan with oil until gently browned.
- Cover the pan and put the chicken stock, salt, and pepper.
- Heat for five min on moderate heat or till fennel is soft.
- Remove the cover and simmer until the fluid has completely evaporated.
- Combine the fennel fronds and parmesan cheese in a mixing bowl.
- Carve the pork loaf and add the fennel to the plate.

Nutrients Calories: 481kcal, Carbs: 55g, Protein: 50g, Fat: 7g

19. Turkey Chili Lean and Green

Prep Time: 7mins

Cook Time: 33mins

Servings: 4

Lean: 2

Green: 3

Condiments: 1

Ingredients

- 2 stalks of onion diced
- 1 tsp of Oil
- 1 diced Red Bell Pepper
- 1/4 tsp of Salt
- 2 oz shredded Cheddar Cheese Reduced-Fat
- 1 diced Jalapeno Peppers
- 2 minced Garlic Cloves
- 1 can of diced Tomatoes Fire-roasted
- 11/4 lbs. of Lean Ground Turkey
- 2 tsp of Cumin
- 4 oz of avocado sliced
- 2 tsp of Chili Powder

Instructions

- Sauté the white portion of the onions with peppers & salt for 2-3mins in a soup pot on moderate heat.
- Cook for 1 minute after adding the garlic.
- Cook till the turkey is heated through, breaking it up into tiny pieces with a wooden spoon.
- Mix in the cumin, tomatoes, and chili powder until everything is well blended.
- Cover and cook on low until 10-15mins.
- Pour it into serving bowls with roughly 1 ounce of avocado & cheese.
- Top with the green portion of the onions.

Nutrients Calories: 452kcal, Carbs: 40g, Protein: 43g, Fat: 15g

20. Spaghetti Lean and Green Squash Bolognese

Prep Time: 20mins

Cook Time: 30mins

Servings: 4

Lean: 2

Green: 3

Condiments: 2

Ingredients

- 1/2 tsp. of Salt
- 1 Spaghetti Squash
- 11/4 lbs. of Lean Beef
- 2 stalks of Scallions minced
- 1 cup of Tomatoes diced
- 2 tbsp Parmesan Cheese Low-fat
- 1 cup of Water
- 1/2 tsp. of Salt
- 1 tbsp. of Paprika
- 1/2 tsp. of Black Pepper

Instructions

- Preheat the oven at 400 degrees Fahrenheit.
- Pull out seeds from spaghetti squash by cutting them in half.
- Cook spaghetti squash onto a baking sheet for approximately 30mins, or till the flesh can be easily torn with a fork.
- So, when squash is done, take it out of the oven & remove the flesh into a dish with a spoon or fork.
- Take 3 cups and set aside any leftovers for another supper.
- Toss the 3-cup spaghetti squash with salt and basil leaves to blend.
- In a saucepan, mix your ground beef, scallions, tomatoes, water, pepper, paprika, and salt whilst squash continues cooking.
- Boil it, stirring frequently, over medium-high moderate heat.
- Turn down the heat to low and cook for approximately 30mins after the mixture starts to boil.

Nutrients: Calories: 320kcal, Carbs: 14g, Protein: 32g, Fat: 16g

21. Skillet Philly Lean and Green Cheese Steak

Prep Time: 10mins

Cook Time: 25mins

Servings: 5

Lean: 2

Green: 1

Condiments: 3

Ingredients

- 1/2 cup of chopped Green Onions
- 1 1/2 lbs. of chopped Beef Steak
- 1 cup sliced Orange Bell Pepper
- 1 cup sliced Yellow Bell Pepper
- 1 1/2 cups of Provolone Cheese Low-fat
- 1 cup sliced Red Bell Peppers
- 1 Garlic Cloves
- 1 tbsp. of Soy Sauce Low Sodium
- 2 tsp. of Ground Ginger

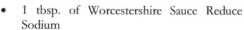
- 1 tbsp. of Worcestershire Sauce Reduce Sodium
- 3 tbsp. of Ketchup Reduced Sugar
- 2 tsp. of Sriracha

Instructions

- Preheat the oven at 400 degrees Fahrenheit.
- Prepare beef steak by chopping it into pieces of bite-size.
- Cook in a pan that has been gently coated with cooking spray over high heat.
- Maintain a high enough temperature to sear the meat steak.
- Rotate often when cooking; after the meat is browned, take it from the pan but cover it to keep it warm.
- Add the onions to the same pan.
- Cook on high heat until the edges are gently browned.
- Remove onions from the pan and lay them on the beefsteak that has been cooked, covering the skillet to keep it warm.
- If necessary, add water to same skillet.
- Heat the peppers over high, turning often, until the edges become slightly browned.
- Take the onions out from the pan and top with the peppers, and cover to keep heat.
- Heat for 30 seconds with the garlic inside the pan before adding the soy sauce, ginger, Sriracha, Worcestershire sauce and ketchup.
- Let it simmer for 5min. Return the onions, steak, and peppers along with the seasonings.
- Still need to put it all together. Provolone cheese should be sprinkled on top.
- Preheat the oven to 350°F and bake for 5mins.
- Turn oven to broil after 5mins, then cook for about 2 minutes, or until the cheese melt and is lightly browned.
- To avoid burning the cheese, keep an eye on it.

Nutrients: Calories: 724kcal, Carbs: 8g, Protein: 72g, Fat: 44g

22. Lean and Green Soup Beef Noodles

Prep Time: 5mins

Cook Time: 25mins

Servings: 4

Lean: 2

Green: 3

Condiments: 3

Ingredients

- 1 tsp. of Oil
- 2 1/2 cups of Zucchini
- 3 Baby Bok halved Choy
- 6 cups Beef Broth Low Sodium
- 1/4 tsp. of Flakes of Red Pepper Crushed
- 2 stalks of diced Spring Onions
- 2 tbsp Reduced Sodium Soy Sauce
- 1 1/4 lbs. Lean Beef sliced
- 1/2 tsp Fresh Ginger Root grated
- 1 tsp Sesame Oil
- 1/4 tsp. of Black Pepper
- 1/4 cup Thai Basil shredded

Instructions

- Heat Baby Bok Choy & spring onions inside a wok with oil.
- Mix soy sauce, broth, and ginger inside a large soup pot.
- Put to a gentle simmer, covered. Put the steak pieces into your soup after slicing it thin.
- Raise the stew to a mild boil, then reduce to a low flame, then cover, and cook till the meat is fully cooked.
- Remove the soup from the heat and stir in the zucchini noodles.
- Combine the sesame oil, black pepper, basil, and flakes of red pepper.
- Serve hot with an equal quantity of soup in each dish.

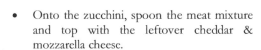

Nutrients: Calories: 345kcal, Carbs: 44g, Protein: 26g, Fat: 7g

23. Lean and Green Casserole Zucchini Pizza

Prep Time: 10mins

Cook Time: 50mins

Servings: 4

Lean: 4

Green: 2

Condiments: 1

Ingredients
- 1/4 tsp. of Salt
- 3 1/2 cups shredded Zucchini
- 2 Eggs
- 1 chopped Green Bell Pepper
- 4 oz shredded Mozzarella Cheese Reduced-Fat
- 1/4 cup of grated Parmesan Cheese
- 4 oz shredded cheddar Cheese Reduced-Fat
- 1/2 lb. of Lean Beef
- 1 can Cooking Spray
- 1 (14.5) oz diced Italian Tomatoes

Instructions
- Preheat the oven to 400 degrees Fahrenheit.
- In a sieve, combine zucchini and salt.
- Allow 10 minutes for moisture to evaporate before pressing.
- Combine eggs, zucchini, parmesan, mozzarella and cheddar cheese.
- In a lightly oiled baking dish, mix the ingredients together.
- Bake about 20 minutes.
- Next, in a pan, sauté the meat and onion till done.
- Drain any excess liquid before adding the tomatoes.

- Onto the zucchini, spoon the meat mixture and top with the leftover cheddar & mozzarella cheese.
- Green peppers go on top.
- Bake for another twenty minutes or until well heated.

Nutrients: Calories: 190kcal, Carbs: 11g, Protein: 13g, Fat: 10g

24. Philly Cheesesteak Lean and Green Peppers

Prep Time: 10mins

Cook Time: 20mins

Servings: 4

Lean: 3

Green: 2

Condiments: 1

Ingredients
- 1/3 cup of Yellow Onion
- 4 Green Bell Peppers
- 2 Garlic Cloves
- 6 oz of mushrooms Baby Bella
- 4, 1 oz of Provolone Cheese
- 1/4 cup of Beef Broth Low Sodium
- 4 tbsp Cream Cheese Low-Fat
- 1 lb. of Roast Deli Beef

Instructions
- Preheat the oven to 400 degrees Fahrenheit.
- Remove the ribs & seeds from the peppers and keep them aside.
- Sauté garlic and onions in the stock in a large pan on moderate heat for approximately 5mins.
- Cook, stirring occasionally, till the mushrooms are soft.
- Heat roast Beef for 3-5 minutes, stirring occasionally.

 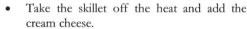 
- Take the skillet off the heat and add the cream cheese.
- Using a quarter piece of cheese, line the interior of every bell pepper.
- Next, spoon 1/8 of the beef mixture into each pepper, and top with some other quarter piece of cheese.
- Rep with the rest of the bell pepper halves.
- Cook for 15-20mins, or until the peppers are soft and the cheese melt.

Nutrients: Calories: 224kcal, Carbs: 10g, Protein: 20g, Fat: 12g

25. Braised Eggplant& Lamb Shanks

Prep Time: 60mins

Cook Time: 60mins

Servings: 4

Lean: 1

Green: 3

Condiments: 2

Ingredients

- 4 12-ounce of lamb shanks
- 1 ½ pounds of eggplant peeled
- 2 tablespoons of ground sumac
- ½ cup = chopped parsley
- ½ teaspoon of pepper
- 1 ¼ teaspoon of salt
- 1 diced green bell pepper
- 2 tablespoons of olive oil, extra-virgin
- 3 minced cloves garlic
- 1 diced onion
- 1 cup of water
- 5 diced plum tomatoes

Instructions

- Set apart the slices of eggplant cut lengthwise into half-inch-wide segments and crosswise into one-inch-wide segments.

- Sumac pepper and salt on lamb shanks.
- In a Dutch oven, heat oil on moderate flame.
- Cook, rotating often, till the lamb is browned on both sides, about 5-7 mins total.
- Place on a platter to cool.
- In the same saucepan, add the oil, onion, bell pepper, garlic cloves, and sumac.
- Heat, stirring often, for 3-5 minutes or until the veggies begin to wilt.
- Put the lamb back in the pot.
- Combine the tomatoes, eggplant, & water in a mixing bowl.
- Bring the water to a boil.
- Lower heat to keep a simmer, then cover, and heat till the lamb is indeed very soft, two days, stirring regularly and flipping the shanks halfway through.
- To preserve lamb warm, transfer it to a platter and cover with foil.
- Increase the heat to moderate and boil the sauce for 5-10mins, or until it has slightly reduced & thickened.
- Remove the pan from the heat and add 1/4 cup parsley.
- In a separate dish, mix the leftover parsley and garlic.
- Garnish with a parsley-garlic combination on top of the lamb & vegetable sauce.

Nutrients: Calories: 321kcal, Carbs: 19g, Protein: 31g, Fat: 3g

26. Lamb Stew

Prep Time: 60mins

Cook Time: 3hrs. 15mins

Servings: 8

Lean: 2

Green: 3

Condiments: 2

Ingredients

- 1 tablespoon of olive oil
- 1 1/2 pounds stew of lamb meat boneless
- 4 teaspoons of ground cumin
- ¼ teaspoon of cayenne pepper
- ¼ teaspoon of salt
- 1 tablespoon of ground coriander
- Ground pepper
- 6 ounces of baby spinach
- 1 can of diced tomatoes
- 1 chopped onion
- ¾ cup of chicken broth reduced-sodium
- 1 can of chickpeas,
- 4 minced cloves of garlic

Instructions

- In a slow cooker, put the lamb.
- In a bowl, combine the oil, coriander, cumin, salt, cayenne, and pepper.
- Stir the lamb in spice paste to thoroughly coat it.
- Onion should be placed on top. In a saucepan on moderate heat, bring the broth, tomatoes, & garlic to boil.
- On the lamb & onion, spoon the sauce.
- Cover and simmer for 3 hours. In a bowl, mash chickpeas.
- Add the mashed & chickpeas, as well as spinach, to your stew.
- Cover and simmer on high for five min or until spinach has wilted.

Nutrients: Calories: 253kcal, Carbs: 12g, Protein: 19g, Fat: 14g

27. Lamb and Rice

Prep Time: 15mins

Cook Time: 10hrs.

Servings: 6

Lean: 1

Green: 2

Condiments: 1

Ingredients

- 1 can of diced tomatoes
- 2 pounds lamb shoulder boneless
- 1 chopped onion
- 1 serrano seeded chili pepper
- Fresh Cilantro
- 6 minced cloves garlic
- 1 teaspoon of ground ginger
- ½ teaspoon of dry mustard
- 1 teaspoon of ground coriander
- ¼ teaspoon of salt
- 2 cups brown rice cooked
- ⅛ teaspoon of cayenne pepper

Instructions

- Remove any excess fat from the lamb and chop it into 2-inch pieces.
- Place the lamb in your slow cooker with a capacity of 3 1/2 to 4 quarts.
- Toss tomatoes, garlic, onion, chili pepper, coriander, ginger, mustard, cayenne pepper and salt in a mixing bowl.
- Pour the mixture over the meat in the slow cooker.
- To blend, stir everything together.
- Cover & cook for 10-12 hours over low heat.
- Serve the lamb on cooked rice with a slotted spoon.
- Remove the fat from the cooking liquid in the cooker and throw it away. Serve with Cilantro as a garnish.

Nutrients: Calories: 330kcal, Carbs: 21g, Protein: 32g, Fat: 12g

28. Lamb Stew

Prep Time: 8mins

Cook Time: 30mins

Servings: 8

Lean: 2

Green: 4

Condiments: 1

Ingredients

- 1 ¾ pound of peeled white potatoes
- 2 pounds of lamb leg, boneless
- 3 leeks
- 3 stalks sliced celery
- ¼ cup of chopped parsley leaves
- 3 carrots
- 1 14-ounce of can chicken broth reduced-sodium
- 1 teaspoon of salt
- 2 teaspoons of chopped thyme
- 1 teaspoon of ground pepper

Instructions

- In a slow cooker, mix the lamb, leeks, potatoes, carrots, broth, celery, salt, thyme, and pepper; mix to incorporate.
- Cover and simmer on low for 8 hours. Before serving, add the parsley.

Nutrients: Calories: 247kcal, Carbs: 26g, Protein: 21g, Fat: 2g

29. Greek Spaghetti

Prep Time: 25mins

Cook Time: 1hr. 15mins

Servings: 10

Lean: 1

Green: 2

Condiments: 1

Ingredients

- 1 yellow onion
- 2 pounds of ground lamb
- 3 crushed cloves garlic
- 1 28-ounce can of crushed tomatoes no-salt-added

- 1 cup of red wine
- 1 cup of water
- Greek Grated hard cheese
- ½ teaspoon of ground pepper
- 1 teaspoon of salt
- ½ teaspoon of ground cinnamon
- 20 ounces of Spaghetti whole-wheat
- ¼ teaspoon of ground allspice
- 1 tablespoon of butter

Instructions

- In a saucepan on moderate heat, cook the lamb till no pinker, 7-8 minutes, turning often & breaking up using a spoon.
- Cook, turning -occasionally, until the onion is transparent, about 4-5 minutes.
- Cook, stirring constantly, for 2-3 minutes or until garlic is soft but just not browned.
- Pour in the wine & scrape away any browned pieces with a spatula.
- Toss in tomatoes with their juice, as well as the salt, cinnamon, pepper, and allspice.
- Bring to low heat, then cook, stirring periodically, for 1 hour.
- Bring a big saucepan of water to one boil approximately twenty minutes before sauce is done. Cook the pasta as directed on the packet.
- Drain thoroughly. Toss in a large mixing dish with the butter until it melts.
- Place on a serving dish and serve.
- Pour the sauce on the Spaghetti and toss to combine.
- If preferred, serve using cheese on top.

Nutrients: Calories: 429kcal, Carbs: 47.g, Protein: 25g, Fat: 14g

31. Lean and Green Spinach Salad with Crusted Pork Chops

Prep Time: 30mins

Cook Time: 21mins

Servings: 4

Lean: 1

Green: 3

Condiments: 2

Ingredients

- 1 tsp of Lime Juice
- 4 oz of Pork Chops
- 2 tsp of Jerk Seasoning
- 8 cups of Baby Spinach
- 1 tsp of Black Pepper
- 1/2 tsp of Salt
- 3/4 cup of Radishes sliced
- 1 tbsp of Lemon Juice
- 1 cup of diced Roma tomatoes

Instructions

- For every pork chop, split the marinated lime juice, jerk spice, black pepper, and a pinch of salt.
- Allow thirty minutes for pork chops to marinate.
- Preheat oven at 450 degrees Fahrenheit.
- Put pork chops in a preheated oven for about 10mins to reach an interior temperature of around 145°F after marinating.
- In a saucepan, heat water while pork is preparing food.
- Cook, stirring occasionally, until spinach starts to wilt, about 1 minute.
- Put the radishes, lemon juice, tomatoes, pepper, & a pinch of salt into the spinach in a mixing bowl right away.
- Allow 10mins for pork chops to rest.
- Garnish your pork chops with a salad of wilted spinach.

Nutrients: Calories: 223kcal, Carbs: 12g, Protein: 22g, Fat: 10g

32. Lean and Green Collard Greens& Parmesan Meatballs

Prep Time: 10mins

Cook Time: 60mins

Servings: 4

Lean: 4

Green: 1

Condiments: 2

Ingredients

- 11/2 cup of Chicken Stock
- 12 cups of chopped Collards Greens
- 1/4 cup of Hemp Seeds
- 11/4 lbs. of Lean Pork
- 1/2 tsp of Salt
- 2 Eggs
- 1/2 tsp of Black Pepper
- 1 tbsp of Balsamic Vinegar
- 2 tbsp Parmesan Cheese Low-fat

Instructions

- Boil 4 cups water in a big saucepan, then include collard greens.
- Cook, covered, for 5 minutes.
- Remove the water from the pot and insert the chicken stock.
- Cook collards with broth for 20 minutes on moderate flame.
- Combine ground pork, salt, eggs, and pepper inside a mixing bowl while collard greens start cooking.
- Form the ingredients into eight meatballs of equal size.
- Simmer for another 20 minutes after adding meatballs into the collards.
- Take the meatballs out and toss the collard greens with the hemp seeds, balsamic vinegar and parmesan.
- Enable approximately 5 minutes of simmering time to allow the flavors to meld.
- Meatballs should be served atop a braised collards bed.

Nutrients: Calories: 310kcal, Carbs: 9g, Protein: 41g, Fat: 13g

33. Slow-Cooker Meal Prep Pork Shoulder

Prep Time: 30mins

Cook Time: 9hrs.

Servings: 12

Lean: 1

Green: 2

Condiments: 1

Ingredients

- 1 tablespoon of olive oil
- 3 pounds of lean pork shoulder boneless
- 1 sliced yellow onion
- Pepper
- 1 teaspoon of cumin
- 10 sliced cloves garlic
- 1 teaspoon of paprika
- ¼ cup of coconut aminos
- ¼ cup of tomato paste
- Salt

Instructions

- Using paper towels, thoroughly dry the pork.
- Heat olive oil in a pan over moderate heat.
- Cook for 4 minutes on each side to brown the pork shoulder.
- Remove the pork shoulder from the pan and put it aside.
- Reduce the heat to low in the skillet.
- Cook, turning occasionally, till the onion is brown in spots and nearly scorched in others, approximately 2 minutes. Garlic, paprika and cumin should be added now.
- Cook for approximately 30 seconds or until aromatic.
- Place the pork shoulder in the slow cooker, then cover with tomato paste.
- Scrape the pan using a rubber spatula to distribute the garlic, onion, and spices on

pork shoulder. Pour the coconut aminos on top of the pork shoulder.
- Salt & pepper to taste. Cook over low for 8-10 hours, covered.
- Using two forks, shred the pork. Before storage, let it cool fully.

Nutrients: Calories: 168kcal, Carbs: 5g, Protein: 21g, Fat: 7g

34. Chimichurri Pork

Prep Time: 30mins

Cook Time: 1hr. 30mins

Servings: 4

Lean: 1

Green: 1

Condiments: 2

Ingredients

- 1 tbsp of dried parsley
- 1 lb. of pork loin boneless roast
- 1 tsp of garlic powder
- 1/2 tsp of salt
- 1 tsp of paprika
- 1/4 tsp of red pepper crushed flakes
- 1/2 tsp of red pepper crushed flakes
- 4 baking potatoes
- 1 tbsp of oil
- 1 cup of sliced mushrooms
- 1 1/2 cups of fresh parsley
- 2 tbsp of oil
- 1/2 cup of fresh Cilantro
- 2 tbsp of oil
- 2 garlic cloves
- 2 tbsp of red wine vinegar

Instructions

- Combine the garlic powder, dried parsley, salt, paprika, oil and red pepper flakes in a bowl to make pork roast rub.

- Spread the rub across the pork roast till it is evenly distributed.
- Refrigerate the pork roast for an hour after covering it.
- Mix the potatoes & mushrooms along with some oil on a wide baking sheet, diced into 1" chunk.
- Place the roast, with potatoes & mushrooms, in the center of baking sheet, then roast until it reaches an interior temperature of 145 degrees F.
- Make the chimichurri sauce whilst pork is prepared.
- Put the Cilantro, parsley oil and roasted garlic in a food processor and process till a coarse sauce form.
- Blend in the vinegar & red pepper flakes unless you've achieved the desired texture.
- Take the roast out from oven, slice it thinly, and arrange with chimichurri sauce on the side.

Nutrients: Calories: 336kcal, Carbs: 5g, Protein: 28g, Fat: 22g

35. **Pork Broccolini Thai-Style Stir Fry**

Prep Time: 14mins

Cook Time: 56mins

Servings: 4

Lean: 1

Green: 2

Condiments: 2

Ingredients
- 1–2 tbsp of sesame oil
- 1 lb. of pork loin
- 2 chopped garlic cloves
- 1/4 cup of coconut sugar
- 1–2 tbsp of tamari gluten-free
- 2 tbsp of fish sauce
- 1/3 cup nuts chopped
- Thai basil leaves
- 1/3 c cup of red onion
- 1/4 tsp of ground ginger
- Sea salt & pepper
- 1/4 tsp of chili flakes of red pepper
- 2 bunch broccolini stalks
- 1 Thai red pepper sliced
- 1 tbsp of lime juice
- 1 or 2 shisoto pepper sliced

Instructions
- First, ensure your meat and vegetables are clean and cut.
- Garlic should be chopped or minced.
- Set everything aside and heat oil in a frying pan to moderately high.
- Toss in the meat and garlic.
- Cook for another 2-3 minutes or until the meat is well browned.
- Remove the pan from the heat.
- Add the spices, sugar, and soy sauce or gluten-free tamari to same pan.
- Cook, stirring often, until the sugar & sauce begin to bubble & caramelize.
- Approximately 2 to 3 minutes. Return the pork, nuts, salt, onion, broccolini, and pepper to the pan, then stir fry for about 3-five min.
- Continue tossing your meat/veggies into sugar sauce when frying with other tablespoons of tamari sauce.
- Stir in sliced peppers & lime juice, and cook for another 1-two min on moderately high, stirring constantly. Place everything on a plate.
- Keep the sauce aside. Several tablespoons of sauce should be poured over each plate or serving bowl, & fresh Thai basil should be garnished.

Nutrients: Calories: 358kcal, Carbs: 25g, Protein: 29g, Fat: 16g

36. Paleo Keto Pistachio Pesto with Pork Tenderloin

Prep Time: 15mins

Cook Time: 15mins

Servings: 4

Lean: 1

Green: 0

Condiments: 1

Ingredients

- 1 1/2 cups of fresh basil
- 1/3 Cup of Roasted Shelled Salted Pistachios
- 1/2 Cup of Packed Cilantro
- Zest half a lemon
- 1 Tbsp of lemon juice
- 1 Tbsp of Water
- Salt and pepper
- Salt & pepper
- 3 Tbsp of Olive Oil
- 4 Zucchinis, spiralized
- 2 lb. of Pork tenderloin
- Salt
- 1 1/2 Tbsp of Olive oil

Instructions

- Preheat the oven at 400 degrees Fahrenheit. Sprinkle the pork using pepper and salt after rubbing it with olive oil.
- In oven baking pan, heat the olive oil over moderate flame.
- Cook the pork on both sides until golden brown.
- Place the pan in oven and cook for 10-fifteen min.
- Remove pork from oven, then cover, and set aside to rest for ten min.
- Process some pistachios inside a food processor or until they are coarsely chopped.
- Combine the basil, lemon juice, Cilantro, and lemon zest in a mixing bowl. Process until everything is finely minced and mixed.
- Stream in water & olive oil while the machine is running until the mixture is creamy and well combined.
- Preheat a big skillet over medium heat. Cook, tossing occasionally, till the zoodles are tender and gently browned.
- Spread zoodles out on paper towel onto the counter.
- Place a second paper towel on the top of zoodles and push quite as much liquid out as possible.
- Toss the zoodles with the pesto sauce until fully incorporated.
- Garnish with sliced pork, lemon juice, and more pistachios, if preferred, and serve.

Nutrients: Calories: 486kcal, Carbs: 9.7g g, Protein: 50g, Fat: 27g

37. Paleolithic Noodles with Sweet Potato Lo Mein

Prep Time: 20mins

Cook Time: 20mins

Servings: 4

Lean: 1

Green: 3

Condiments:1

Ingredients

- 1 tsp of olive oil
- 3 sweet potatoes
- 1/8 tsp of salt
- 1 tsp of apple cider vinegar
- 1 lb. of pork chops boneless
- 2 tsp of pure sesame oil
- 2 tsp of coconut aminos
- 1 tsp of olive oil
- 1 red bell pepper

- 1 cup of white mushrooms
- 1 tsp of tapioca flour
- 2 bunches of baby bok choy green and white parts
- 1 Tbsp of ginger minced
- 3 cloves of garlic minced
- 3 scallions of green and white
- 1/3 cup of coconut aminos
- 1/2 cup of carrots shredded
- 2 Tbsp of sesame oil pure

Instructions

- Before you begin, make sure you have all of your ingredients cut, sliced, & ready to cook.
- To begin, combine the sliced pork] with the marinade ingredients in a mixing dish and put it aside.
- Prepare the sweet potato noodles & vegetables.
- Preheat the oven at 400 degrees, then prepare a baking sheet for your noodles.
- Spread out the noodles equally after tossing them with oil and salt.
- Roast for 20 minutes. Next, heat olive oil in a nonstick pan over high temperature.
- When the pan is hot, insert the pork and cook, moving constantly to ensure uniform browning for 1 min or less.
- Transfer to a platter, leaving juices inside the pan, and leave aside as you stir-fry the vegetables.
- Keep the temperature on high, then add all of the vegetables, ginger, garlic, a scallion to the pan, cooking and stirring for several minutes till fork tender and starting to brown.
- In a bowl, mix the sauce components for the following step.
- Reduce the heat to medium-low and pour in the sauce mixture, tossing to combine.
- Boil it to thicken sauce, then mix in the pork to coat in sauce, then take off the heat.
- When the noodles are done, add them to the mix and toss lightly to integrate everything.

- Serve immediately with finely sliced green scallions as a garnish. Approximately 4-6 servings.

Nutrients: Calories: 337kcal, Carbs: 25g, Protein: 22g, Fat: 15g

38. Lean and Green Eggplant Puree with Grilled Zucchini and Seared Tofu

Prep Time: 15mins

Cook Time: 30mins

Servings: 4

Lean: 3

Green: 2

Condiments: 1

Ingredients

- 1 tsp. of salt divided
- 1 lb. of eggplant halved
- 1/2 tsp. of Black Pepper
- 1 tbsp. of Parmesan Cheese
- 31/2 lbs. of sliced tofu Extra Firm
- 1 can of Cooking spray
- 2 tsp. of Olive Oil, Extra Virgin
- 1 Zucchini
- 1/4 cup of Peanut Butter, Powdered
- 2 tsp. of Balsamic Vinegar
- 1 tsp. of garlic crushed

Instructions

- Preheat the oven at 425 degrees Fahrenheit. Cut eggplant.
- Place the eggplant onto a baking sheet that has been gently oiled and sprinkled with salt.
- Roast your eggplant for approximately 30 minutes. The flesh is facing up.
- Cut the tofu into thick slices and put it in a dish while eggplant roasts.
- Season the tofu pieces with a quarter tsp of salt and black pepper.
- Allow for 20-30 minutes of marinating time.
- Toss zucchini using 1 tsp olive oil & 1/4 tsp salt & pepper after cutting it on the diagonal into slices.
- Grill and turn zucchini until golden brown on both sides.
- Remove from the oven & keep warm.
- Take the eggplant out from oven after it has done roasting and allow it to cool.
- Fill a food processor halfway with the meat.
- Combine the garlic, oil, salt and powder of peanut butter in a mixing bowl.
- Set it aside & keep warm after processing into a thick purée.
- Caramelize the tofu pieces in an oiled nonstick pan until light brown.
- Place the zucchini, tofu, and eggplant mixture on a platter in a neat circle.
- Finish with a drizzle of balsamic vinegar as well as a sprinkling of Parmesan cheese.

Nutrients: Calories:301 kcal, Carbs:19 g, Protein:17 g, Fat:20 g

39. Lean and Green Watercress & Roasted Eggplant with Grilled Tempeh

Prep Time: 10mins

Cook Time: 25mins

Servings: 4

Lean: 1

Green: 3

Condiments: 2

Ingredients

- 41/2 cup of Eggplant
- 20 oz. of Tempeh
- 1/2 tsp. of Rice Vinegar
- 1 tsp. of Lime Juice
- 1/2 tsp. of salt divided
- 1/2 tsp. of Black Pepper
- 11/2 cup of Watercress
- 1/2 tbsp. of Lemon Juice
- 1/4 cup of Scallions diced
- 11/2 tbsp. of Soy Sauce Reduced Sodium

Instructions

- Allow for thirty min of soaking by pouring boiling water on the tempeh to soak it by two inches.
- Combine the pepper, eggplant, rice vinegar, and salt in a bowl.
- Preheat the oven at 425°F, then roast the chopped eggplant for 20-30mins.
- Remove eggplant from oven and combine with the scallions, watercress, lemon juice, tomatoes, and salt right away.
- Take the tempeh out from water, then dry it with a paper towel.
- It should be sliced into quarter-inch pieces. 2 mins on every side, grill, sear cut tempeh till golden brown.
- Pour soy sauce & lime juice over grilled tempeh over eggplant salad.

Nutrients: Calories: 283kcal, Carbs:43 g, Protein: 8g, Fat:9 g

40. Lean and Green Kimchi Stew & Napa Cabbage

Prep Time: 10mins

Cook Time: 20mins

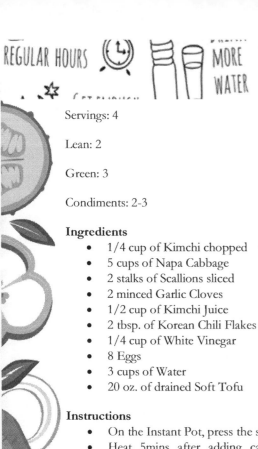

Servings: 4

Lean: 2

Green: 3

Condiments: 2-3

Ingredients

- 1/4 cup of Kimchi chopped
- 5 cups of Napa Cabbage
- 2 stalks of Scallions sliced
- 2 minced Garlic Cloves
- 1/2 cup of Kimchi Juice
- 2 tbsp. of Korean Chili Flakes
- 1/4 cup of White Vinegar
- 8 Eggs
- 3 cups of Water
- 20 oz. of drained Soft Tofu

Instructions

- On the Instant Pot, press the sauté button.
- Heat 5mins after adding cabbage, garlic, Kimchi, and Korean chili flakes.
- Combine the vinegar, kimchi juice, and water in a bowl.
- Secure the cover, change the setting to stew, and set the timer to ten min.
- When Instant Pot sounds, let the pressure out normally.
- Open the cover and crack one egg at one time into the pan.
- Cook eggs to get desired texture by pressing the sauté button one more.
- Cut tofu after draining and drying it with a cloth.
- Cook for a few more minutes after adding the tofu.
- Serve in dishes with scallions on top.

Nutrients: Calories: 379kcal, Carbs:49 g, Protein:17 g, Fat:14 g

41. Lean and Green Zucchini Noodles and Vegetarian Meatballs

Prep Time: 5mins

Cook Time: 5mins

Servings: 1

Lean: 1

Green: 1

Condiments: 1

Ingredients

- 4 spiraled Zucchini
- 2 tbsp. of Olive Oil
- 1 lb. of Vegan Meatballs
- 1/4 cup of Fresh chopped Basil
- 1 cup of Rao's Homemade Sauce

Instructions

- Vegan meatballs should be heated as directed on the package in microwave.
- In a pan, heat the olive oil on moderate flame. Put zucchini noodles into hot olive oil and toss until softened, about 2-3 mins.
- Lower the heat and toss the zucchini noodles with Rao's Homemade Sauce. Allow 2 to 3 mins for noodle sauce mixture until boil. Before serving, add the hot meatballs into sauce noodle combination & heat for2 minutes.
- Serve with a basil garnish on top of each dish.

Nutrients: Calories:324 kcal, Carbs:13 g, Protein:15 g, Fat:25 g

42. Tofu Stir Fry Lean & Green

Prep Time: 9mins

Cook Time: 6mins

Servings: 1

Lean: 1

Green:4

Condiments: 2

Ingredients
- Onion 1/4 cup
- Tofu 1/2 cup
- Mushroom 1/4 cup
- Cherry tomato 1/4 cup
- 1 teaspoon Oil
- 1 cup Baby spinach
- Green chili 1 teaspoon
- Salt
- Hot sauce
- Black pepper

Instructions
- To begin, prepare a nonstick tawa over moderate heat, then sauté with nonstick spray or oil.
- After that, add chopped onions & cook for several minutes till they become translucent. After that, add the mushrooms and stir-fried until softened.
- Put tofu cubes into this and cook for 1-2 minutes. Now add spinach & tomatoes, then toss everything together completely.
- Cook for 3–4 minutes. Season to taste with salt & pepper. Mix in the spicy sauce well.

Nutrients: Calories:162 kcal, Carbs:11 g, Protein: 12g, Fat:9 g

43. Sautéed Garlic with String Beans

Prep Time: 15mins

Cook Time: 10mins

Servings: 6

Lean: 1

Green: 0

Condiments:2

Ingredients
- 1 tbsp. of olive oil
- 1/4 tsp. of black pepper
- 2 pounds of trimmed string beans
- 1/2 tsp. of kosher salt
- 3 tbsp. of chopped garlic

Instructions
- A big container of water should be brought to one boil.
- Cook for two mins, then strain and put aside string beans.
- On moderate flame, heat a big skillet.
- Stir in some olive oil, garlic, and string beans.
- Stir in salt & pepper, then whisk in the remaining garlic until string beans are well covered. Cook for five min.

Nutrients: Calories:68 kcal, Carbs:8 g, Protein: 2g, Fat:4 g

44. Zucchini Fritters, Baked

Prep Time: 30mins

Cook Time: 10mins

Servings: 10

Lean: 1

Green: 2

Condiments: 2

Ingredients
- 1 finely diced shallot
- 1 1/2 pounds of zucchini
- 2 eggs
- 1/4 cup of crumbled goat cheese
- 1/2 cup of almond flour
- 1/4 tsp. of pepper

- Salt & pepper
- 1 cup of yogurt
- 2 tbsp. of olive oil
- 2 minced garlic cloves
- 1/2 tsp. of salt
- 1 tbsp. of chopped chives

Instructions

- Zucchini should be grated and placed in a bowl.
- Season with salt, mix well and set aside for twenty minutes.
- Zucchini will be drained of moisture as a result of salt. In a basin, crush zucchini. Transfer the zucchini into a clean dish after squeezing off the liquid with a cheesecloth.
- Combine the eggs, shallot, almond flour, goat cheese, salt, & pepper in a large bowl. Then mix everything with a swirl. In a mixing dish, combine the ingredients for the zucchini fritters in a skillet. Heat oil on moderate flame.
- Chunk out mounds of the ingredients into the heated pan using a spoon. Press down every fritter with a spoon to compress it.
- Cook fritters for 3 to 4 mins on every side. Take the fritters from pan and blot away any excess oil using a paper towel. In a mixing dish, mix the sauce components and whisk until smooth. In a separate bowl, make garlic chive yogurt sauce.
- Serve with dollop of your sauce on top of the fritters, and enjoy.

Nutrients: Calories: 113kcal, Carbs:5 g, Protein:5 g, Fat:9 g

45. Vegetable Frittata Slice

Prep Time: 20mins

Cook Time: 30mins

Servings: 4

Lean: 1

Green: 4

Condiments: 0

Ingredients

- 7 Eggs
- 6 cups of leaves of Baby spinach
- 15 g Plain flour
- 1 Carrot
- 1 chopped Red capsicum
- 1 Zucchini
- 3 crushed Garlic cloves,
- ½ thinly sliced Red onion

Instructions

- Preheat the oven to 180 degrees Celsius. Using baking paper, coat ovenproof dish using oil. Place the spinach inside a basin, cover, then microwave for 1-2 minutes.
- Allow it to cool before draining, squeezing away any extra liquid, and coarsely chopping. In a basin, lightly beat the eggs.
- Combine spinach, zucchini, carrots, capsicum, garlic, onion, and flour in a bowl. Stir in the pepper and salt. Spread the mixture evenly in the prepared dish. Bake for thirty min.
- Allow for 5 minutes in the dish before chopping it into four pieces to serve.

Nutrients: Calories:250 kcal, Carbs:8 g, Protein:8 g, Fat:12 g

46. Cauliflower Fritters and Spiced Pumpkin with Salsa

Prep Time: 15mins

Cook Time: 25mins

Servings: 4

Lean: 0

Green: 3

Condiments: 1

Ingredients

- 200 g Cauliflower
- 400 g peeled pumpkin
- ½ cup Panko breadcrumbs
- 2 tsp Ground coriander
- ½ tsp chili flakes Dried
- ¼ cup chopped coriander
- Oil spray
- 2 Tomatoes chopped
- 1 chopped Red capsicum
- 2 sliced green shallots
- 1 tbsp Lime juice
- 1 tsp grated lime rind
- 1½ cup Rocket

Instructions

- In a steamer, steam pumpkin & cauliflower for about 10–12 mins.
- Take them to a large mixing bowl & mash well. Sprinkle with salt and toss in panko, ground coriander, chili flakes, and fresh coriander. To tighten up these patties, form the mixture in twelve patties, then refrigerate for 30 minutes.
- Inside a bowl, mix the capsicum, remaining coriander, tomatoes, lime zest, shallots, and juice to form the salsa. Set aside after seasoning with pepper and salt. Heat a big frying pan on moderate heat, lightly sprayed with oil.
- Cook for three mins on every side in batches. Serve each diner three fritters with salsa & rocket just on side.

Nutrients: Calories: 444kcal, Carbs:25 g, Protein:28 g, Fat:24 g

47. Pumpkin Falafels

Prep Time: 20mins

Cook Time: 40mins

Servings: 4

Lean: 2

Green: 1

Condiments: 1

Ingredients

- 2 400g-can of canned chickpeas
- 1 chopped Red onion
- 750 g roasted Pumpkin,
- 1½ tsp Ground cumin
- 3 Garlic cloves
- 1½ tsp Ground coriander
- Oil spray
- 2 tbsp chopped Fresh coriander
- 1 chopped red chili
- 2 tbsp chopped flat-leaf parsley
- 2 tsp Lemon juice
- 150 g 99% plain yogurt fat-free

Instructions

- Preheat the oven to 220 degrees Celsius. Preheat a nonstick pan on moderate flame, lightly sprayed with oil.
- Cook, stirring occasionally, for 8 to 10 minutes. Remove the pan from the heat and put it aside. In a stick blender, pulse chickpeas till a chunky puree develop. In a mixing basin, mash the pumpkin.
- Combine the onion, 2\3 garlic, chickpeas, cumin, chili, coriander, and cut herbs in a large bowl. Make 12 balls out of the mixture and lay them on a baking pan. Allow 20 minutes for chilling.
- Falafels should be baked for 20 to 30 minutes. In a small bowl, mix the lemon juice, yogurt, and leftover garlic to create the Dressing.
- Falafels should be served with a yogurt dressing.

Nutrients: Calories: 66kcal, Carbs:7 g, Protein: 3g, Fat:3 g

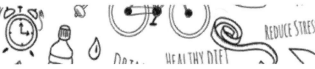
48. Lentil and Carrot Patties

Prep Time: 20mins

Cook Time: 20mins

Servings: 4

Lean: 1

Green: 1

Condiments: 1

Ingredients

- 250 g chopped Potato
- 300 g chopped Orange sweet potato
- Oil spray
- 2 grated Carrots
- ¼ cup Light sour cream
- 1 400g can of canned Lentils
- 2 tbsp chopped Fresh mint

Instructions

- Cook sweet potato & potato until they are soft. Drain. In a mixing basin, mash the potatoes. Mix in your carrots & lentils.
- Salt & pepper to taste. Form your mixture in 12 patties with moist hands. Heat a big nonstick frying skillet over moderate heat, lightly sprayed with oil.
- Cook about four minutes on each side. In a small mixing bowl, mix sour cream & mint.
- Serve your patties with a dollop of mint sour cream on top.

Nutrients: Calories: 382kcal, Carbs:36 g, Protein: 14g, Fat: 17g

49. Cauliflower Feta and Capsicum Crust Pizza

Prep Time: 20mins

Cook Time: 35mins

Servings: 4

Lean: 1

Green: 2

Condiments: 3

Ingredients

- ½ cup of mozzarella cheese
- ½ cauliflower
- ⅔ cup Plain flour
- 2 tsp chopped fresh oregano
- 2 Eggs
- Oil spray
- ½ tsp Garlic powder
- ⅔ cup feta cheese Reduced fat
- 1 cup Roasted capsicum
- 2 Green shallots sliced
- 10 chopped Black olives

Instructions

- Preheat the oven at 220 degrees Celsius.
- Spray a baking pan liberally with oil. In a stick blender, combine the cauliflower florets. Process until you get a rice-like consistency. Place in a large mixing basin. Combine the flour, mozzarella, oregano, eggs, and garlic in a mixing bowl. Season to taste with pepper and salt, then toss to blend.
- On the prepared pan, spoon the crust dough into 2 20cm rounds. To make a layer, flatten with a spatula. Bake approximately twenty minutes.

- Flip it over with care. Bake for another 10 minutes. Roasted feta, olives, capsicum, and shallots should be sprinkled over the crust.
- Bake until five min. Serve.

Nutrients: Calories: 74kcal, Carbs: 4g, Protein:6 g, Fat: 4g

50. Pumpkin Mash with Vegetable Tray Bake

Prep Time: 15mins

Cook Time: 1hr.

Servings: 4

Lean: 1

Green: 5

Condiments: 2

Ingredients
- 1 Eggplant
- 1 Red capsicum
- 1 Red onion
- 1 Zucchini
- 200 g Mushrooms
- 3 Tomatoes
- 2 crushed Garlic cloves
- Oil spray
- ¾ tsp Ground paprika
- 2 tsp Balsamic vinegar
- 1 tsp Stock powder, gluten-free, vegetable
- 1200 g Butternut pumpkin
- ¼ cup Fresh coriander

Instructions
- Preheat the oven to 180 degrees Celsius. On a lined tray, arrange the capsicum, onion, eggplant, zucchini, mushrooms, and tomatoes.
- Season using salt & pepper after lightly spraying with oil, sprinkling with paprika & garlic, then drizzling with balsamic vinegar.

- Toss to evenly coat the veggies. Bake for about 50 to 60 minutes. In a big pot, combine the pumpkin & stock powder.
- Boil it with water to cover it. Cook for twenty minutes, covered. Drain, then return the pumpkin to the pot & mash well. Salt & pepper to taste.
- Serve the roasted veggies with mashed potatoes and coriander on top.

Nutrients: Calories:159 kcal, Carbs:26 g, Protein:4 g, Fat:5 g

51. Zoodle Bolognese

Prep Time: 10mins

Cook Time: 25mins

Servings: 4

Lean: 2

Green: 5

Condiments: 3

Ingredients
- 1 Onion, chopped
- 500 g beef mince Extra lean
- 1 crushed Garlic clove
- 450 g Tomato passata
- 400 g Canned tomatoes, diced
- Oil spray
- 1½ tbs Tomato paste
- 1 Beef stock cube, gluten-free variety
- 1 tsp Dried herbs
- basil 1 tbsp, leaves
- Zucchini 3, spiralized

Instructions
- Heat a pan on moderate flame, lightly sprayed with oil. Cook for 5 mins.
- Toss in the passata, tomatoes, mixed herbs and tomato paste in pan and boil, stirring constantly. Add the stock cube & stir one more.

- Reduce heat to low and cook for 15 to 20 minutes. When the sauce is almost done, gently oil a big frying pan and put it on moderate heat.
- Cook, stirring occasionally, for 1 to 2 minutes. Season with salt and pepper to taste, then split among dishes and garnish with sauce.
- Serve with basil.

Nutrients: Calories: 417kcal, Carbs: 27g, Protein: 36g, Fat:21 g

Chapter no. 6 Seafood Recipes

1. Lean and Green Swai Fish Baked with Feta & Tomatoes

Prep Time: 10mins

Cook Time: 20mins

Servings: 4

Lean: 2

Green: 3

Condiments: 2

Ingredients
- 2 1/2 tbsp of Olive Oil
- 4 stalks of Scallions chopped
- 2 Garlic Cloves
- 1/4 tsp of Dried Oregano
- 1 cup of Basil Leaves
- 2 1/2 cups of Diced Tomatoes
- 3 Zucchini
- 1/2 tsp of Black Pepper
- 1/2 tsp of Kosher Salt
- 1/3 cup of Feta Cheese Crumbled Reduced-Fat
- 1 3/4 can of Swai Fish

Instructions
- Preheat the oven to 425 degrees Fahrenheit.
- Cook garlic & white portions of the scallions inside 1 tbsp olive oil inside a saucepan till fragrant.
- Cook, stirring occasionally, for twenty minutes.
- Cut zucchinis. Remove the tomatoes from the heat and mix in the green portion of the scallions.
- Place the chopped zucchini in oven-safe casserole dish & top with the Swai fish.
- Drizzle the leftover olive oil over the Fish and sprinkle with salt & 1/4 tsp pepper.
- Cooked tomatoes & feta cheese go on top of Swai fish.
- Bake for twenty minutes. Finish with basil & black pepper.

Nutrients: Calories: 427kcal, Carbs: 24g, Protein: 50g, Fat: 13g

2. Lean and Green Swai Fish Grill Mates with Zucchini and Eggplant

Prep Time: 10mins

Cook Time: 25mins

Servings: 1

Lean: 1

Green: 1

Condiments: 2

Ingredients

- 1 tsp of McCormick Grill Mates Fiery 5 Pepper Seasoning
- 7 oz of Swai Fish
- 1 can of Cooking spray
- 1 sliced Zucchini
- 1/2 tsp of Black Pepper
- 2 slices of Eggplant

Instructions

- Preheat your outside grill to high.
- Coat the tin foil using cooking spray. Put McCormick Grill Mates Fiery 5 Pepper Seasoning.
- Put the Swai piece of Fish onto a large tin foil, large enough even to wrap it around.
- Bring the long ends of foil together all the way up and across the Swai fish.
- To make a seal & prevent the fold from breaking apart, bring foil sides close.
- Arrange the zucchini & eggplant pieces in a grill basket with a grill basket.
- Sprinkle black pepper. Close grill cover after placing Swai fish & grill basket with veggies on it.
- Following 15 minutes, examine the Swai fish whether it is done or not. After fifteen min, flip the veggies in grill basket. Cook for another 10 minutes.

Nutrients: Calories: 434kcal, Carbs: 23g, Protein: 27g, Fat: 22g

3. Lean and Green Swai Fish Savory Cilantro

Prep Time: 80mins

Cook Time: 35mins

Servings: 2

Lean: 1

Green: 3

Condiments: 2

Ingredients

- 2 tbsp Lemon juice
- 4 cup Cilantro
- 2 tbsp Lime Juice
- 1 tsp of Cumin
- 2 tbsp of Red Pepper Hot Sauce
- 1/2 tsp of Salt
- 1 can of Cooking spray
- 4 (7) oz of Swai Fish
- 1/2 cup of Water
- 2 cups of Yellow sliced Bell Pepper
- 2 cups of Green sliced Bell Peppers
- 2 cups of Red sliced Bell Peppers
- 1/2 tsp of Black Pepper

Instructions

- Put Cilantro, lemon/lime juice, cumin, hot red pepper sauce, salt, & water inside a food processor; blend until smooth.
- Fill a resealable bag halfway with the marinade.
- In a separate bowl, combine Swai fish with the marinade. Close the bag press out all the air.
- Chill for one hour, flipping the bag every now and then.
- Preheat the oven to 400°F once the meat has marinated.
- In an oiled, square baking sheet, lay all slices of pepper into a thin layer and season with pepper & the rest salt. Cook for twenty minutes, rotating the pepper slices halfway through.
- Drain the Swai fish and toss out the marinade.
- Using the remaining chopped, Cilantro, crust the tops of the Swai fish. Place the Swai fish on the pepper slices, then bake for 12-14 mins.

Nutrients: Calories: 198kcal, Carbs: 1g, Protein: 16g, Fat: 12g

4. Lean and Green Shrimp Salad Ceviche Avocado

Prep Time: 10mins

Cook Time: 5mins

Servings: 2

Lean: 1

Green: 2

Condiments: 3

Ingredients

- 2 tbsp Lime Juice
- 1/4 cup of Green Onions
- 1 tsp of Olive Oil
- 1 tbsp chopped Fresh Cilantro
- 1/4 tsp of Black Pepper
- 1/8 tsp of Salt
- 1.5 cups diced whole Tomatoes
- 1/4 cup of diced Jalapeno Peppers
- 4.5 oz diced Avocado
- 14 oz chopped Cooked Shrimp

Instructions

- Mix olive oil, lime juice, salt, green onions, and pepper inside a bowl.
- To bring out the aromas of the onions, marinate them for 5mins.
- Combine tomato, avocado, jalapeño peppers, and prepared shrimp inside a bowl.
- Mix all of the components in a large mixing bowl, then add Cilantro & gently stir to combine.
- Taste and season with the leftover pepper and salt.

Nutrients: Calories: 95kcal, Carbs: 4g, Protein: 12g, Fat: 4g

5. Lean and Green Shrimp Bites

Prep Time: 10mins

Cook Time: 6mins

Servings: 3

Lean: 1

Green: 2

Condiments: 2

Ingredients

- 21 oz of Cooked Shrimp
- 2 tsp of Olive Oil
- 1 tbsp sliced Creole seasoning
- 1/2 cup of chopped Green Onions
- 6 oz of Avocado
- 2 cups of cucumber sliced
- 2 tbsp chopped Fresh Cilantro
- 1/4 tsp of Salt
- 1/4 tsp of Cayenne Pepper
- 2 tsp Lemon juice

Instructions

- Cucumbers should be sliced. Set it aside 6 ounces of mashed avocado, Cilantro, green onion, salt, pepper, & lemon juice for avocado sauce.
- Preheat olive oil & creole seasoning inside a pan on high heat.
- Cook for 2-3 mins, until shrimp are slightly browned.
- Make the bites by layering avocado sauce, cucumber slices, then shrimp on top.

Nutrients: Calories: 220kcal, Carbs: 20g, Protein: 9g, Fat: 8g

6. Lean and Green Shrimp with Spaghetti Squash

Prep Time: 10mins

Cook Time: 0mins

Servings: 2

Lean: 4

Green: 1

Condiments:1

Ingredients
- 1 tbsp Cream Cheese
- 1/2 cup Chicken Broth Low-Sodium
- 7 oz of Cooked Shrimp
- 3-slice Cheese Wedge
- 1/4 tsp Seasoning of Old Bay
- 1/4 cup of Water
- 1 cup of Cooked chopped Spaghetti Squash
- 1/2 cup chopped Broccoli

Instructions
- Combine cheeses, water, chicken broth, & Old Bay seasoning into a blender.
- In a large mixing bowl, combine the broccoli & spaghetti squash.
- Mix in some cooked shrimp gently.

Nutrients: Calories: 190kcal, Carbs: 4g, Protein: 31g, Fat: 9g

7. Lean and Green Shrimp with Spiralized Zoodles

Prep Time: 15mins

Cook Time: 5mins

Servings: 1

Lean: 1

Green: 1

Condiments: 2

Ingredients
- 7 oz of Cooked Shrimp

- 2 tsp of Olive Oil
- 1 tbsp of Grated Parmesan
- 1 cup spiraled Zucchini
- 1/4 cup of Rao's Marinara Sauce
- 1 cup spiraled Yellow Squash
- 1/2 tsp of Italian Seasoning
- 1/4 tsp of Garlic Salt

Instructions
- Two tsp olive oil, heated in a pan over moderately high heat.
- Cook until 2 minutes. Combine the shrimp, garlic salt, marinara sauce, and Italian seasoning inside a mixing bowl.
- Cook for about 2 minutes.
- Place on a platter and top some parmesan cheese.

Nutrients: Calories: 318kcal, Carbs: 16g, Protein: 49g, Fat: 6g

8. Lean and Green Zucchini Noodles with Garlic Shrimp

Prep Time: 15mins

Cook Time: 7mins

Servings: 1

Lean: 2

Green: 1

Condiments: 0

Ingredients
- 2 tsp of Olive Oil
- 9 oz of Raw Shrimp
- 1 tbsp of Parmesan Cheese
- 1/2 tbsp of Light Butter
- 1.25 tsp of Lemon juice
- 1 tsp of Garlic minced
- 1/2 tsp Parsley chopped
- 1/2 cup of Grape Tomatoes

- 1/8 tsp Red Pepper Crushed Flakes
- 1 cup of Zucchini Noodles

Instructions

- One teaspoon olive oil in a big pan over moderate heat, then put the shrimp & cook for around 4-5 minutes.
- Mix in the Garlic, butter, lemon juice, parsley, red pepper flakes, and tomatoes when the shrimp has become pink.
- In a separate pan, heat 1 tablespoon olive oil over medium heat, add zucchini noodles, cooking for 1-two min.
- Place zucchini noodles on a plate, top with shrimp mixture, & 1 tablespoon Parmesan cheese.

Nutrients: Calories: 214kcal, Carbs: 3g, Protein: 24g, Fat: 11g

9. Lean and Green Salmon Grill Mates with Zucchini and Eggplant

Prep Time: 10mins

Cook Time: 25mins

Servings: 1

Lean: 1

Green: 2

Condiments: 1

Ingredients

- 1 tsp of McCormick Grill Mates Fiery 5 Pepper Seasoning
- 7 oz of Raw Salmon Filets
- 1 can of Cooking spray
- 1 Zucchini sliced
- 1/2 tsp of Black Pepper
- 2 slices of Eggplant

Instructions

- Preheat your outside grill to high.
- Coat the tin foil using cooking spray. 1 tsp. McCormick Grill Mates 5 pepper Fiery, sprinkle.
- Place the salmon on a sheet of aluminum foil large enough to cover around the fillet, skin side down.
- To make a seal & prevent fold from breaking apart, fold sides of foil together.
- Place the zucchini & slices of Eggplant in the grill basket using grill basket.
- Sprinkle some black pepper.
- Close the grill cover and place the salmon & grill basket, and veggies on grill.
- Following fifteen min, examine the salmon for proper cooking; it'll be done when it becomes light pink & reasonably robust to the feel when squeezed.
- After fifteen min, flip the veggies in grill basket. Cook for another ten min.

Nutrients: Calories: 278kcal, Carbs: 25g, Protein: 25g, Fat: 7g

10. Lean and Green Salmon Savory Cilantro

Prep Time: 80mins

Cook Time: 35mins

Servings: 4

Lean: 1

Green: 3

Condiments: 2

Ingredients

- 2 tbsp Lemon juice
- 4 cup Cilantro
- 2 tbsp Lime Juice
- 1 tsp of Cumin
- 2 tbsp of Red Pepper Hot Sauce
- 1 can of Cooking spray
- 1/2 tsp of Salt

- 4 (7) oz of Raw Salmon Filets
- 1/2 cup of Water
- 2 cups of Yellow sliced Bell Pepper
- 2 cups of Green sliced Bell Peppers
- 2 cups of Red sliced Bell Peppers
- 1/2 tsp of Black Pepper

Instructions

- Put ½ cilantro, lemon/lime juice, pepper sauce, salt, cumin, and water in a food processor or blender; blend until smooth.
- Fill a large airtight plastic bag halfway with the marinade.
- In a separate bowl, combine the salmon with the marinade.
- Flip gently to coat salmon after sealing the bag and squeezing the air out.
- Chill for one hour, flipping the bag every now and then.
- Preheat the oven to 400°F once the meat has marinated.
- In an oiled baking dish, lay all slices of pepper in a thin layer and season with pepper & the remaining salt.
- Bake approximately 20 minutes, rotating the pepper slices halfway through.
- Drain the salmon and toss out the marinade.
- Using the remaining fresh cilantro crust, the tops of the Fish.
- Place the salmon on top of the pepper slices, then bake for 12-14 minutes.

Nutrients: Calories: 335kcal, Carbs: 19g, Protein: 35g, Fat: 13g

11. Lean and Green Grilled Shrimp & Zoodles with Dressing of Lemon Basil

Prep Time: 10mins

Cook Time: 12mins

Servings: 2

Lean: 1

Green: 1

Condiments: 2-3

Ingredients

- 2 ½ of cups Zucchini
- 1 lb. of Raw Shrimp
- 1/8 tsp of Salt
- 1/2 cup of Cherry Tomatoes
- 1/8 tsp of Black Pepper
- 1 tbsp of Lemon Zest
- 3/4 cup of Basil
- 1 Garlic Cloves
- 1/4 cup of Almonds sliced
- 1 Shallot chopped
- 2 tsp of Olive Oil
- 1/4 tsp of Red Pepper Crushed Flakes

Instructions

- In blender, mix almonds, garlic clove, shallot, some red pepper flakes, olive oil, lemon zest and red wine vinegar to make the dressing of lemon basil.
- Shake on medium speed until smooth & evenly blended.
- Season some salt & pepper and leave aside.
- To toast the additional almonds, place them in a pan over moderate heat.
- Shake the pan once every second till the almonds are lightly browned.
- Take the almonds off the fire and put them aside.
- 1 tbsp oil, heated over moderate flame Season the shrimp with pepper and salt.
- Heat shrimp for six to eight minutes, or until completely cooked and pink, then mix with 2 heaping spoonful of lemon basil dressing.
- Set aside the seasoned shrimp in a separate clean dish.
- Cut zucchini in thin spaghetti-like strands using a vegetable spiralizer.
- In same pan as the shrimp, put the zucchini noodles, then cook for two minutes on moderate heat.

- Sprinkle zucchini noodles using pepper and salt, and mix with 2 heaping tablespoons of dressing lemon basil. Turn off the heat.
- Any leftover lemon basil dressing may be used in another dish.
- Toss the zucchini noodles, prepared shrimp, and cherry tomatoes gently.
- Toss in the toasted almonds and serve. Serve right away.

Nutrients: Calories: 460kcal, Carbs: 12g, Protein: 9g, Fat: 11g

12. Lean and Green Feta & Tomatoes with Baked Cod

Prep Time: 10mins

Cook Time: 20mins

Servings: 4

Lean: 2

Green: 1

Condiments: 2

Ingredients
- 2 1/2 tbsp of Olive Oil
- 4 stalk chopped Scallions
- 2 Garlic Cloves
- 1/4 tsp of Dried Oregano
- 2 1/2 cups of Diced Tomatoes
- 3 Zucchini
- 1 cup Basil Leaves
- 1/2 tsp of Black Pepper
- 1/2 tsp of Kosher Salt
- 1/3 cup Feta Cheese Crumbled Reduced-Fat
- 1 3/4 can of Cod Fillet

Instructions
- Preheat the oven to 425 degrees Fahrenheit.
- Cook garlic & white portions of scallions in 1 tbsp olive oil inside a saucepan till fragrant.
- Cook, stirring occasionally, for twenty minutes.
- Cut zucchinis. Remove the tomatoes from the heat and mix in the green portion of the scallions.
- Place the Fish cut zucchini in oven-safe casserole dish.
- Drizzle the olive oil over the Fish and sprinkle with salt and pepper.
- Cooked tomatoes & feta cheese go on top of the Fish.
- Bake for approximately 20 minutes.
- Finish with basil and the last of the black pepper.

Nutrients: Calories: 287kcal, Carbs: 9g, Protein: 34g, Fat: 13g

13. Lean and Green Curry Coated Salmon with Napa Cabbage Chili Braised

Prep Time: 7mins

Cook Time: 23mins

Servings: 4

Lean: 2

Green: 2

Condiments: 0

Ingredients
- 1/4 tsp of Salt

- 4 Skinless Boneless Salmon fillets
- 1 1/2 tbsp of Curry Powder
- 2 stalks of minced Green Onions
- 2 tsp minced Ginger Root
- 1 1/4 lbs. of chopped Napa Cabbage
- 1/4 tsp of Red Pepper Crushed Flakes
- 1 cup Chicken Broth Low Sodium

Instructions

- Preheat the oven to 425 degrees Fahrenheit.
- Rub salt into the Fish until it is completely dissolved.
- Allow 5 minutes for the salmon to rest.
- On a dish, spread curry powder, then roll every salmon fillet.
- Place the salmon onto a baking tray, then bake for 8 - 10 mins at 425°F.
- Cut the Napa cabbage and lay it aside when the salmon bakes.
- Put chicken broth & ginger in a pan and broil.
- Cover & boil with cabbage & red pepper flakes.
- Reduce the heat to low and cook for 3-5 minutes.
- Combine the cabbage and green onions in a mixing bowl.
- Serve salmon over cabbage bed.

Nutrients: Calories: 400kcal, Carbs: 7g, Protein: 38g, Fat: 24g

14. Lean and Green Shrimp and Chicken Gumbo

Prep Time: 20mins

Cook Time: 30mins

Servings: 3

Lean: 2

Green: 3

Condiments: 2

Ingredients

- 1 chopped Scallions
- 1 tbsp of Canola Oil
- 2 stalks of Celery diced
- 2 cups of Water
- 1.5 cups of Diced Tomatoes
- 1 Red diced Bell Pepper
- 1/4 tsp of Dried Thyme
- 1/4 tsp of Cayenne Pepper
- 1 Bay Leaf
- 1.5 cups of chopped Okra
- 2 cups Riced Cauliflower
- 1 lb. of Skinless Boneless Chicken Thighs
- 3/4 lbs. of Raw Shrimp
- 1/4 tsp of Black Pepper
- 1/4 tsp of salt

Instructions

- In a saucepan, heat the oil, then add the scallions, Garlic, bell pepper and Celery; sauté till translucent.
- Simmer for fifteen min after adding the water, tomatoes, bay leaf, thyme, and cayenne.
- Continue to cook for another 10 minutes after adding the Okra & chicken.
- Simmer for about 5 min before adding the cauliflower & shrimp. If the gumbo is excessively thick, thin it out with water as needed.
- Season to taste with salt & pepper.

Nutrients: Calories: 160kcal, Carbs: 14g, Protein: 12g, Fat: 5g

15. Garlic Butter Shrimp

Prep Time: 5mins

Cook Time: 15mins

Servings: 4

Lean: 0

Green: 0

Condiments: 1

Ingredients

- 1/4 teaspoon of Seasoning of Stacey Hawkins Dash of Desperation
- 1 3/4 pounds of shrimp
- Nonstick spray
- 1/4 cup chicken stock
- 1 tablespoon of Seasoning of Stacey Hawkins Garlic & Spring Onion
- Juice of 1 lemon
- 8 teaspoons of butter

Instructions

- Put a sizable pan on medium heat and coat with nonstick spray. Combine with shrimp as well as a dash of desperation.
- Cook for 2 to 3 minutes, tossing periodically, until pink. Put the shrimp on a bowl and let it alone.
- In skillet, add Garlic & spring onion, then sauté for about a minute or until fragrant.
- Add lemon juice & chicken stock after stirring.
- Until the water is decreased by half, boil it, then lower the heat. Add butter and stir till melted.
- Add the shrimp, then gently incorporate by stirring.
- Serve warm, topped with parsley as you wish.

Nutrients: Calories: 217kcal, Carbs: 8g, Protein: 30g, Fat: 9g

16. Lean and Green Shrimp and Fried Cauli Rice

Prep Time: 20mins

Cook Time: 10mins

Servings: 4

Lean: 2

Green: 3

Condiments: 2

Ingredients

- 2 Eggs beaten
- 2 tbsp of Canola Oil
- 4 beaten Egg Whites
- 1/4 tsp of Salt
- 2 tbsp Soy Sauce Reduced Sodium
- 1/4 tsp of Black Pepper
- 2 stalks minced Scallions
- 2 minced Garlic Cloves
- 1 1/2 lbs. of Raw Shrimp
- 1 cup of Green chopped Beans
- 1 cup of Green diced Bell Peppers
- 4 cups Riced Cauliflower

Instructions

- Heat Canola oil over moderate heat in a nonstick pan.
- Scramble the egg in the pan. Take from the heat and add salt & pepper.
- Heat the Canola oil in the nonstick pan on the stovetop.
- Cook for 1-2 minutes, until the Garlic & scallions are fragrant.
- Cook for 2 minutes after adding the shrimp.
- Cook for one minute after adding the bell pepper & green beans.
- Toss in the cauliflower & soy sauce.
- After the shrimp and veggies have finished cooking, mix in the scrambled eggs.
- Serve by dividing the mixture into four equal pieces.

Nutrients: Calories: 309kcal, Carbs: 9g, Protein: 30g, Fat: 16g

17. Lean and Green Mahi Mahi Grilled with Jicama Slaw

Prep Time: 20mins

Cook Time: 10mins

Servings: 4

Lean: 1

Green: 3

Condiments: 1-2

Ingredients

- 1 tsp of Salt
- 1 tbsp of Lime Juice
- 1 tsp of Black Pepper
- 2 tbsp of Olive Oil, Extra Virgin
- 4(8oz.) Mahi Mahi Fillets
- 1 cup of Alfalfa Sprouts
- 2 tsp Olive Oil Extra Virgin
- 1 cup sliced Cucumber
- 3 cups sliced Jicama
- 2 cups chopped Watercress

Instructions

- In a bowl, mix 1 teaspoon lime juice, pepper and salt, and oil.
- Brush it on mahi-mahi fillets.
- Cook the Mahi-mahi for 5mins on every side on moderate heat until done.
- Jicama, cucumber, Watercress, & alfalfa sprouts are combined in a dish for the slaw.
- In a bowl, combine lime juice, Salt & pepper, and extra virgin olive oil.
- Drizzle the dressing over the slaw, then toss to mix.

Nutrients: Calories: 320kcal, Carbs: 10g, Protein: 44g, Fat: 11g

18. Lean and Green Shrimp and Rice Sushi of Avocado Cauliflower

Prep Time: 15mins

Cook Time: 5mins

Servings: 2

Lean: 1

Green: 2

Condiments: 1

Ingredients

- 1 tbsp of Rice Vinegar
- 2 ½ cups Riced Cauliflower
- 1/8 tsp sugar substitute Zero-calorie
- 1 1/2 tbsp of Sesame Seeds
- 1/3 cup Greek Yogurt Non-Fat
- 12 oz chopped Shrimp
- 2 tsp of Sriracha
- 1/2 Cucumber sliced
- 1/2 Avocado
- 4 large sheets Nori

Instructions

- Heat cauliflower rice for about five min in a moderate microwave-safe bowl, stirring midway through.
- Set aside after adding the rice vinegar & sugar replacement.
- Set aside diced shrimp, Greek yogurt, and sriracha inside mixing dish.
- Assemble the sushi rolls; Place one nori sheet on a sushi rolling mat, then evenly distribute one 1/4 of cauliflower rice combination over the 1\2 sheet.
- Place the ingredients horizontally over cauliflower rice, keeping some cauliflower rice visible both around and behind them.
- Roll sushi by burying all of the contents into first full roll by sliding the sides of visible Nori nearest to you on the filling. Roll.
- With a clean knife, cut the rolls into pieces. Sesame seeds may be sprinkled on top.

Nutrients: Calories: 129kcal, Carbs: 3g, Protein: 8g, Fat: 8g

19. Salmon Florentine Lean and Green

Prep Time: 15mins

Cook Time: 20mins

Servings: 4

Lean: 2

Green: 3

Condiments: 0

Ingredients

- 1 tsp of Olive Oil
- 1/2 cup of chopped Green Onions
- Cooking Spray
- 2 minced Garlic Cloves
- 1 1/2 cup chopped Cherry Tomatoes
- 1(12) oz chopped Spinach
- 1/4 tsp Red Pepper Crushed Flakes
- 1/4 tsp of Black Pepper
- 1/4 tsp of Salt
- 4 oz of Salmon
- 1/2 cup of Ricotta Cheese

Instructions

- Preheat the oven to 350 degrees Fahrenheit.
- Fry onions in oil inside a medium pan until soft, approximately 2 minutes.
- Cook for another minute after adding the Garlic.
- Add the cherry tomatoes, salt, red pepper flakes, and pepper to the spinach.
- Cook for 2 minutes, stirring occasionally.
- Remove it from heat, then set aside for 10mins to cool.
- Add the ricotta cheese and mix well. Top every salmon fillet with a 1/4 spinach mixture.
- Bake for about 15mins on an oiled baking sheet.

Nutrients: Calories: 472kcal, Carbs: 17g, Protein: 75g, Fat: 12g

20. Lean and Green Red Pepper Roasted Sauce with Zucchini Noodles and Scallops

Prep Time: 5mins

Cook Time: 15mins

Servings: 2

Lean: 1

Green: 2

Condiments: 2

Ingredients

- 1/2 cup of Almond Milk Unsweetened
- 1jar oz of Red Peppers Roasted
- 2 oz of Avocado
- 1 lb. of Scallops
- 1 Garlic Cloves
- 2 tsp of Lemon Juice
- 1/4 and 1/8 tsp of Salt
- 1/2 tbsp of Unsalted Butter
- 2 Zucchini

Instructions

- Blend the red pepper, avocado, milk, lemon juice, red pepper, salt and Garlic in a blender until smooth.
- Puree until completely smooth. In a pan, cook roasted red pepper sauce on moderate flame, stirring periodically, until well heated, approximately 3-5 minutes.

- Put zucchini noodles, toss to combine, and simmer for another 3-5 minutes.
- Meanwhile, in a pan on moderate heat, melt the butter.
- Sprinkle scallops with salt. Cook scallops for 1-2 minutes per side.
- Scallops should be served over zucchini noodles.

Nutrients: Calories: 273kcal, Carbs: 14g, Protein: 10g, Fat: 21g

21. Low-Carb Lean and Green Lobster Roll

Prep Time: 15mins

Cook Time: 5mins

Servings: 2

Lean: 2

Green: 2

Condiments: 1-2

Ingredients
- 1 tbsp melted Unsalted Butter
- 4 Romaine Lettuce
- 1/3 cup Greek Yogurt Non-Fat
- 12 oz of Cooked Lobster
- 1 stalk of chopped Celery finely
- 2 tbsp of Mayonnaise Olive Oil
- 2 tsp of Lemon Juice
- 1/4 tsp of Seasoning of Old Bay
- 1 tbsp Chives chopped
- 1/4 tsp of Black Pepper
- 1/4 tsp of salt

Instructions
- Preheat the grill to 400 degrees.
- To make a boat-like form for lobster filling, cut romaine lettuce hearts into half lengthwise.
- Brush the insides & edges of every boat using butter, then grill to gently sear the lettuce.
- Combine all other ingredients inside a medium-sized mixing bowl, except the lobster meat, in a mixing bowl.
- Fold in your lobster flesh until it is totally covered after all of the ingredients have been well blended.
- Serve immediately by dividing the lobster mixture equally among boats and garnishing with lemon slices.

Nutrients: Calories: 237kcal, Carbs: 40g, Protein: 23g, Fat: 26g

Chapter no. 7 Fueling Hacks Recipes (Smoothies & Shakes, Icy, Salty, Crunches, Soft Bakes, Pancakes)

1. Lean and Green Biscuit Pizza

Prep Time: 5mins

Cook Time: 15mins

Servings: 1

Lean: 2

Green: 0

Condiments: 1

Ingredients
- 1/4 cup of Cheese, Reduced-Fat
- 2 tbsp. of Cold Water
- 1 sachet Herb Biscuit Buttermilk Cheddar
- 2 tbsp. of Rao's Homemade Sauce
- 1 can of Cooking spray

Instructions
- Preheat the oven at 350 degrees Fahrenheit.
- Combine the biscuit mix & water in a tiny, thin, round crust form on a baking sheet that has been lightly coated using cooking spray. 10mins in the oven.
- After cooking for 10mins, cover with tomato sauce & mozzarella, then bake for another 4-5 minutes.

Nutrients: Calories: 162kcal, Carbs: 44g, Protein: 13g, Fat: 18g

2. Lean and Green Mint Thin Cookies

Prep Time: 10mins

Cook Time: 15mins

Servings: 4

Lean: 2

Green: 0

Condiments:1

Ingredients
- 2 bars of Cookie Crisp Bars
- 2 sachets of Chocolate Brownie
- 1/4 tsp. of Mint Extract
- 1 tablespoon of Egg Substitute
- 2 tbsp. of Cashew Milk
- 2 tbsp. of Almond Milk, Unsweetened

Instructions
- Preheat the oven at 350 degrees Fahrenheit.
- Soften Mint Chocolate Cookie Crispy Bars in the microwave for about 15-20 seconds.
- Combine the Decadent Dual Chocolate Brownies, fluid egg replacement, milk, and mint essence in a mixing bowl.
- Microwave crunchy bars should be added at this point.
- On a baking sheet, form the batter into 8 cookie-shaped chunks.

- Preheat oven to 350°F and bake for about 12-15 minutes.

Nutrients: Calories: 74kcal, Carbs: 2g, Protein: 5.5g, Fat: 5g

3. Lean and Green Peanut Butter Mini Cups

Prep Time: 15mins

Cook Time: 0mins

Servings: 2

Lean: 2

Green: 0

Condiments: 0

Ingredients
- 1/4 cup of Peanut Butter, Powdered
- 10 tbsp. of Vanilla Almond Milk, Unsweetened
- 2 sachets of Chocolate Brownie
- 10 tbsp. of Cashew Milk

Instructions
- Mix Decadent Dual Chocolate Brownie and 6 tbsp almond milk in a mixing bowl till smooth; leave aside.
- Mix powder of peanut butter with the leftover almond milk in a separate dish until smooth & creamy.
- Place the brownie & peanut butter mixes in different sealable bags, moderate to large in length.
- To make piping bags, slice a little bit off one end of every bag.
- Fill the bottom 3rd of 20 holes in a tiny round silicone baking mold with brownie batter.
- In the middle of every slot, pipe a little quantity of peanut butter on top of a brownie.

- Fill each hole with the leftover brownie batter, which should be piped on base of peanut butter to coat it. Freeze for 2 hours or until firm.

Nutrients: Calories: 220kcal, Carbs: 26g, Protein: 2g, Fat: 13g

4. Lean and Green Orange Spiced Cranberry Cheesecake

Prep Time: 9mins

Cook Time: 1mins

Servings: 4

Lean: 1

Green: 0

Condiments: 0

Ingredients
- 1 1/2 cups of Greek Yogurt, Low-fat
- 1 tsp. of Orange Zest
- 4 sachets of OPTAVIA Cranberry Nut Honey Chili Bars
- 2 tbsp. of Cheesecake Pudding, Sugar-free

Instructions
- Using 8 cupcake wrappers, line a basic muffin tray.
- Every Honey Chili Cranberry Nut Bar should be cut in half. Microwave the bar pieces crunch-side downwards on a tray for 20-30 seconds.

Nutrients: Calories: 218kcal, Carbs: 19g, Protein: 3g, Fat: 15g

5. Tiramisu Milkshake Lean and Green

Prep Time: 5mins

Cook Time: 0mins

Servings: 1

Lean: 2

Green: 0

Condiments: 0

Ingredients
- 1/2 cup of Ice
- 1 sachet of OPTAVIA Soft Serve Treat Frosty Coffee
- 2 tbsp. of Whipped Topping Pressurized
- 6 oz Greek Yogurt. Non-Fat
- 1/2 cup of Cashew Milk
- 1/2 cup of Almond Milk Unsweetened
- 2 tbsp. of Chocolate Syrup, Sugar-free

Instructions
- In a mixer, combine all of the components and mix until smooth.
- Pour the mixture into a mason jar.
- Drizzle with maple syrup and finish with whipped cream.

Nutrients: Calories: 630kcal, Carbs: 82g, Protein: 16g, Fat: 27g

6. Lean and Green Cheesecake Mint Chocolate Muffins

Prep Time: 10mins

Cook Time: 0mins

Servings: 4

Lean: 1

Green: 0

Condiments: 0

Ingredients
- 12 oz of Greek Yogurt, Low-fat
- 8 Mint Leaves

- 4 sachets of Cookie Crisp Chocolate Mint Bars
- 1/4 tsp. of Peppermint Extract
- 2 tbsp. of Chocolate Pudding Sugar-free Mix

Instructions
- 8 cupcake liners should be lined in a basic muffin tray.
- Every Chocolate Mint Cookie Crisp Bar should be cut in two.
- Microwave the bar pieces crunch-side downwards on a microwave-safe tray for 20-30 seconds.
- Press it down every piece into the base of a cupcake mold to produce a thin crust.
- Continue until all of the cupcake liners have been filled.
- Mix low-fat regular Greek Yogurt and fat-free, sugar-free chocolate pudding mixture in a mixing bowl until thoroughly blended.
- Divide the yogurt and pudding mix evenly among the muffin liners. Freeze for 30-60 minutes.
- If preferred, garnish with mint leaves & serve right away.

Nutrients: Calories: 274kcal, Carbs: 32g, Protein: 8g, Fat: 12g

7. Caprese Lean and Green Pizza Bites

Prep Time: 8mins

Cook Time: 12mins

Servings: 4

Lean: 2

Green: 1

Condiments: 1

Ingredients

- 1/2 cup of Almond Milk, Unsweetened
- 4 sachets of Cheddar Herb Buttermilk Biscuit
- 2 tbsp. of Balsamic Vinegar
- 2 tsp. of Olive Oil
- 1 cup of Basil Leaves
- 1 can of Cooking spray
- 3 sliced Roma tomatoes
- 4 oz chopped Mozzarella Log

Instructions

- Preheat the oven at 450 degrees Fahrenheit.
- Combine milk, Buttermilk Cheddar Herb Biscuit, and oil in a moderate mixing dish.
- In a basic-sized, gently muffin tray, split biscuit mixture equally among the 12 holes.
- Each muffin pan slot should be layered with a piece of mozzarella, a piece of tomato, and several basil leaves.
- Bake for about 10-12 minutes.
- Before serving, drizzle the tops using balsamic vinegar.

Nutrients: Calories: 115kcal, Carbs: 1g, Protein: 12g, Fat: 5g

8. Lean and Green Pinto's and Cheese

Prep Time: 3mins

Cook Time: 1mins

Servings: 1

Lean: 1

Green: 0

Condiments: 3

Ingredients

- 1/8 tsp. of Cayenne Pepper
- 1 sachet Sour Cream and Chives Mashed Potatoes
- 2 tsp. of Cholula Hot Sauce
- 1 tbsp. of shredded Cheddar Cheese Reduced-Fat
- 1 tsp. of Cumin

Instructions

- Prepare the OPTAVIA Sour Cream and Chives Smashed Potatoes according to the package directions.
- Mix in the cumin & cayenne pepper completely.
- Enjoy it with Cholula & cheddar cheese.

Nutrients: Calories: 272kcal, Carbs: 18g, Protein: 2g, Fat: 19g

9. Fruit Popsicles

Prep Time: 5mins

Cook Time: 0mins

Servings: 6

Lean: 1

Green: 0

Condiments: 0

Ingredients

- 2 ½ cups of fruit
- ½ tsp. of lemon juice
- ¾ cup of Yogurt
- ¼ tsp. of vanilla extract
- 4-6 honey

Instructions

- In the sequence stated, put all components to the container.
- Blend on high for 50 to 70 seconds.

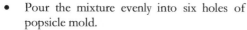

- Pour the mixture evenly into six holes of popsicle mold.
- Place the mold in your freezer, then secure the covers and sticks over the top.
- Chill for eight hours.
- Remove the molds from the freezer and run them beneath water for thirty seconds before releasing the popsicle.

Nutrients: Calories: 260kcal, Carbs: 19g, Protein: 7g, Fat: 13g

10. Cheesy Spinach Lean and Green Smashed Potatoes

Prep Time: 5mins

Cook Time: 5mins

Servings: 1

Lean: 1

Green: 1

Condiments: 1

Ingredients

- 1 cup of Baby Spinach
- 1 tsp. of Grated Parmesan
- 1 sachet of OPTAVIA Essential Creamy Smashed Roasted Garlic Potatoes
- 1/2 cup of mozzarella cheese shredded reduced-fat
- 1 tsp of water

Instructions

- Follow the package instructions for making Roasted Garlic Creamy Smashed Potatoes.
- Heat spinach for about one minute with a little water.
- Combine the mozzarella, spinach, & parmesan cheese with the Roasted Garlic Creamy Smashed Potatoes.

Nutrients: Calories: 166kcal, Carbs: 16g, Protein: 10g, Fat: 4g

11. Real Fruit Icy Poles

Prep Time: 5mins

Cook Time: 0mins

Servings: 6

Lean: 0

Green: 0

Condiments: 0

Ingredients

- 2 cups of 99% fruit juice
- 1 cup of fruit like mango, strawberries, cherries, blueberries, kiwifruit, watermelon, pineapple

Instructions

- Cut the fruit into bits and fill the ice pole molds approximately halfway.
- Fill the mold to the brim with fruit juice.
- Freeze for at least 24 hours. Run some hot water on the mold and carefully slip the frozen pole out while serving.

Nutrients: Calories: 235kcal, Carbs: 31g, Protein: 2g, Fat: 12g

12. Yoghurt Icy Poles

Prep Time: 10mins

Cook Time: 0mins

Servings: 8

Lean: 1

Green: 0

Condiments: 1

Ingredients

- ⅓ cup of maple syrup

- One cup frozen or fresh mixed berries
- 2 cups of Greek Yogurt
- Five passion fruits
- ½ tsp. of vanilla extract

Instructions

- Set some ice poles/popsicle molds on the bench to get started. Before you begin, double-check that the freezer has enough space.
- Combine the sugar, Yogurt, and vanilla in a mixing bowl and whisk until sugar is completely dissolved.
- Cut the mixture in half and divide it between two bowls.
- Mix the fruit pulp into one of the bowls holding the yogurt mixture.
- Mash the berries inside a food processor for another half.
- Fill the second yogurt dish with the berry mixture.
- To generate a swirl look, stir, but don't entirely blend.
- Place the individual bowls in various ice pole molds and freeze until frozen.

Nutrients: Calories: 234kcal, Carbs: 12g, Protein: 4g, Fat: 21g

13. Lean and Green Buffalo and Chicken Meatballs

Prep Time: 15mins

Cook Time: 30mins

Servings: 4

Lean: 2

Green: 1

Condiments: 2

Ingredients

- 1 1/4 lbs. of Lean Ground Chicken

- 3 Multigrain Crackers
- 3 Celery diced
- 1/4 cup of Ranch Dressing Low-Fat
- 1/2 tsp. of Garlic Powder
- 1 Egg
- 1/2 cup of Buffalo Wing Sauce
- 1/2 tsp. of Onion Powder

Instructions

- Preheat the oven at 350 degrees Fahrenheit.
- Mix crackers into breadcrumb bits in a stick blender.
- Form the ingredients into twelve meatballs, lay them on a prepared baking sheet, & bake for about 30mins at 350°F.
- Serve with celery sticks & salad dressing.

Nutrients: Calories: 207kcal, Carbs: 11g, Protein: 17g, Fat: 10g

14. Coconut Colada Lean and Green

Prep Time: 5mins

Cook Time: 2mins

Servings: 0

Lean: 2

Green: 0

Condiments: 1

Ingredients

- 6 oz of Coconut Milk Unsweetened
- 1 sachet of Creamy Vanilla Shake
- 1/2 cup of Ice
- 6 oz of Ginger Ale
- 1/4 tsp. of Rum Extract
- 4 tbsp. of Coconut Milk Unsweetened

Instructions

- Mix coconut milk, OPTAVIA Essential Creamy Vanilla Shake, coconut, diet ginger ale, rum essence, and ice inside a blender.

115

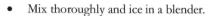
- Mix thoroughly and ice in a blender.
- Fill 2 Pina colada mugs halfway with the contents and cover with the coconut.
- Serve right away.

Nutrients: Calories: 5kcal, Carbs: 9g, Protein: 0g, Fat: 0g

15. Neapolitan Froyo Lean and Green Popsicles

Prep Time: 25mins

Cook Time: 0mins

Servings: 6

Lean: 2

Green: 0

Condiments: 0

Ingredients
- 1 cup of Cashew Milk
- 1 cup of Vanilla Almond Milk Unsweetened
- 1 packet of sugar substitute, Zero-calorie
- 2 cups of Yogurt divided Low-fat
- 1 sachet of Creamy Vanilla Shake
- 1 sachet of Creamy Chocolate Shake
- 1 sachet of Wild Strawberry Shake

Instructions
- Inside blender, combine 1/3 cup milk, Creamy Chocolate Shake, plain Greek Yogurt, & sugar replacement; mix until smooth.
- Place the mix in your freezer for fifteen min after equally distributing it across the base of 6 big popsicle molds.
- Steps 1 to 2 are repeated using Creamy Vanilla Shake and, finally, Wild Strawberry Shake.
- Freeze for 4 hours.

Nutrients: Calories: 169kcal, Carbs: 19g, Protein: 3g, Fat: 9g

16. French Toast Lean and Green Sticks

Prep Time: 15mins

Cook Time: 5mins

Servings: 2

Lean: 1

Green: 0

Condiments: 1

Ingredients
- 2 tbsp. of Cream Cheese Low-Fat
- 2 tbsp. of Syrup Sugar-free
- 2 sachets of Cinnamon Crunchy Cereal
- 1 can of Cooking Spray
- 6 tbsp. of Egg Substitute

Instructions
- Mix Cinnamon Crunchy O's Cereal in a breadcrumb-like texture in a blender.
- Pour the treated Cinnamon Crunchy O's into a big mixing basin, add cream cheese & liquid egg-substitute, then stir till a dough form.
- Make 6 French toast sticking pieces out of dough.
- Slightly Cook the sticks of French toast in a pan sprayed with cooking spray and heat over moderate heat till warm and nicely browned on both sides.

Nutrients: Calories: 210kcal, Carbs: 28g, Protein: 8g, Fat: 8g

17. Lean and Green Peanut Butter Bites with Sugar

Prep Time: 5mins

Cook Time: 0mins

Servings: 1

Lean: 1

Green: 0

Condiments:0

Ingredients
- 2 tbsp. of Peanut Butter Powdered
- 1\2 sugar
- 1 bar of Crisp Bar Peanut Butter
- 1 tbsp. of water

Instructions
- In a bowl, combine the powder of peanut butter with water and sugar to make smooth paste.
- Heat Creamy Double Peanut Butter Crisp Bar for about fifteen seconds.
- To make a dough, combine the heated bits of a bar with some peanut butter.
- Produce 4 bite-sized pieces using your finger.
- Place in the refrigerator till ready to serve.

Nutrients: Calories: 99kcal, Carbs: 14g, Protein: 24g, Fat: 4g

18. Greek Yogurt Lean and Green Breakfast Bark

Prep Time: 10mins

Cook Time: 0mins

Servings: 2

Lean: 1

Green: 0

Condiments: 0

Ingredients
- 1 sachet of Red Berry Crunchy Cereal
- 1-2 packets of sugar substitute Zero-calorie
- 12 oz of Greek Yogurt Non-Fat

Instructions
- Mix Greek yogurt and sugar alternatives in a mixing basin.
- Nonstick foil should be used to line an 8x 8 baking sheet. In the bottom of a baking dish, put Greek yogurt in a uniform layer.
- On top of the Yogurt, spread the Red Berry Crunchy O's Cereal. Freeze for 4–5 hours.
- Using a sharp knife, cut the bark into pieces.

Nutrients: Calories: 25kcal, Carbs: 4g, Protein: 2g, Fat: 0.2g

19. Lean and Green Pecan Muffins of Sweet Potato

Prep Time: 10mins

Cook Time: 20mins

Servings: 4

Lean: 1

Green: 1

Condiments: 0

Ingredients
- 1 cup of Cold Water
- 2 sachets of Honey-sweet Potatoes
- 2 sachets of Spiced Gingerbread
- 1/3 oz. of Pecans chopped
- 1/4 cup of Original Unsweetened
- 6 tbsp. of Egg Substitute
- 1/2 cup of Pumpkin Pie Spice
- 1/2 tsp. of Baking Powder
- 1/2 tsp. of Vanilla Extract
- 1 can of Cooking Spray

Instructions
- Preheat the oven at 350 degrees Fahrenheit. Make Honey Sweet Potatoes as directed on the box.
- Allow to cool slightly before serving.

 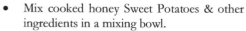 
- Mix cooked honey Sweet Potatoes & other ingredients in a mixing bowl.
- Fill the muffin tray with the mixture and divide it into eight holes.
- Using a lightly sprayed prepared paper cupcake.
- Pecans, chopped, should be sprinkled on top.
- Preheat oven to 350°F and bake for twenty minutes.

Nutrients: Calories: 146kcal, Carbs: 50g, Protein: 3g, Fat: 6g

20. Chocolate Milkshakes

Prep Time: 10mins

Cook Time: 0mins

Servings: 2

Lean: 1

Green: 0

Condiments: 0

Ingredients
- 3 scoops of vanilla ice cream
- ¼ cup of chocolate-flavored syrup
- ¾ cup of milk

Instructions
- Place milk & syrup in a mixer. Cover and mix for 2 seconds at high speed.
- Put ice cream to the mix.
- Cover and combine for five seconds at low speed.
- Pour the mixture into mugs.
- Serve right away.

Nutrients: Calories: 380kcal, Carbs: 41g, Protein: 8g, Fat: 14g

21. Lean and Green Hemp & Coconut Green Smoothie

Prep Time: 5mins

Cook Time: 0mins

Servings: 1

Lean: 1

Green: 1

Condiments: 2

Ingredients
- 1/2 cup of chopped Cucumber
- 1 sachet of Renewal Shake
- 1 cup of Raw Baby Spinach
- 1 stalk of Celery chopped
- 1 Ice
- 1 stalk of Kale
- 1 tbsp. of Hemp Seeds
- 1 tbsp. of Fresh Mint
- 1/2 cup of Refrigerated Coconut Milk, Unsweetened

Instructions
- In blender, combine all components and mix them at high speed for 1 to 2 minutes.

Nutrients: Calories: 229kcal, Carbs: 21g, Protein: 11g, Fat: 11g

22. Strawberry Smoothie

Prep Time: 5mins

Cook Time: 5mins

Servings: 4

Lean: 1

Green: 0

Condiments: 0

Ingredients

- 1/3 cup of strawberry jam
- 1 1/2 cups of milk
- 3 cups of frozen strawberries

Instructions

- In a mixer, combine the strawberry jam, chilled strawberries, and milk.
- Cover the top with the lid. Blend until completely smooth.

Nutrients: Calories: 169kcal, Carbs: 32g, Protein: 3g, Fat: 3g

23. Cucumber Cups

Prep Time: 15mins

Cook Time: 0mins

Servings: 10

Lean: 0

Green: 2

Condiments: 2-3

Ingredients

- 1 pt. quartered cherry tomatoes
- 4 cucumbers
- 1/2 c. of crumbled feta
- 1/2 c. chopped kalamata olives
- 1 lemon juice
- Black pepper
- 2 tbsp. of chopped dill
- 1 minced clove garlic
- 1 tsp. of oregano
- 1 tbsp. of olive oil extra-virgin
- kosher salt

Instructions

- Cucumbers should be cut in 3" slices.
- Make a well in every cucumber with a spoon.
- Toss together tomatoes, feta, olives, dill, garlic, lemon juice, olive oil, & oregano

inside a mixing bowl. Salt & pepper to taste. Fill cucumbers with salad mixture.

- If preferred, top with additional dill before serving.

Nutrients: Calories: 68kcal, Carbs: 3g, Protein: 1g, Fat: 4g

24. Hard Boil Eggs

Prep Time: 5mins

Cook Time: 15mins

Servings: 12

Lean: 1

Green: 0

Condiments: 0

Ingredients

- water
- 12 eggs

Instructions

- In a saucepan, crack the eggs, then cover with 1 inch of water.
- Boil in a saucepan on the stove. Turn off the heat, then cover the saucepan immediately.
- Allow for 11 minutes of resting time.
- Remove from the pan and place in a bowl of cold water.
- Allow 2 minutes for cooling before peeling & serving.

Nutrients: Calories: 78kcal, Carbs: 1g, Protein: 6g, Fat: 5g

25. Toast of Ricotta-Honey with Berries

Prep Time: 5mins
Cook Time: 0mins
Servings: 1
Lean: 1
Green: 0

119

Condiments: 0

Ingredients

- 1/3 cup of ricotta
- 2 slices of multigrain bread
- Sea salt
- 1/4 cup of berries
- 1/2 tsp. of honey

Instructions

- Bread should be toasted. Meanwhile, combine the ricotta & honey in a small dish.
- On the bread, apply ricotta, then top fresh berries.
- Additional honey should be drizzled on top, and salt should be sprinkled on top.

Nutrients: Calories: 133kcal, Carbs: 25g, Protein: 7g, Fat: 2g

26. Pistachio and Oat Bars

Prep Time: 13mins
Cook Time: 12mins
Servings: 12
Lean: 0
Green: 1
Condiments: 1-2

Ingredients

- 1 cup of rolled oats
- 1 cup of shelled pistachios
- Chopped pistachios
- ½ teaspoon of sea salt
- 2 tablespoons of olive oil
- ¼ cup of maple syrup
- ⅓ cup of coconut flakes unsweetened

Instructions

- Preheat oven at 350°F and line a baking tray with parchment.
- Mix the oats, pistachios, and salt inside a stick blender till a meal form.
- Drizzle in maple syrup & olive oil, as well as the meal, will start to come all together in a flaky, almost-wet batter.
- Top the dough using coconut flakes & the leftover pistachios & press it firmly into pan.
- Bake for about 10-12 minutes.

- Don't overbake your squares; they should still be a touch soft.
- Holding two edges of parchment paper, carefully remove the dough out of pan.
- It should be cut in squares. If desired, drizzle a very little syrup on top for added sweetness.
- For a week, keep the pieces in an airtight container.

Nutrients: Calories: 100kcal, Carbs: 13g, Protein: 3g, Fat: 4g

27. Feta Dip

Prep Time: 20mins
Cook Time: 0mins
Servings: 8
Lean: 1
Green: 3
Condiments: 2

Ingredients

- 1 cup of Greek Yogurt
- 12 oz. of feta
- 1/4 cup of olive oil, extra-virgin
- 1 oz. of block softened cream cheese
- 1 lemon zest and juice
- Red pepper flakes
- Kosher salt
- Pita chips
- 2 tbsp. of chopped dill
- 1/2 cup of cherry tomatoes
- 1/2 cup of chopped cucumber

Instructions

- Using a hand blender, mix Greek yogurt, feta cheese, oil, cream cheese, lemon zest and juice in a mixing bowl.
- Mix in dill, then season using salt & red pepper flakes.
- Toss the dip with tomatoes, cucumber, dill, and just a splash of oil inside a serving dish.
- Pita chips are a great accompaniment.

Nutrients: Calories: 28kcal, Carbs: 0.8g, Protein: 1g, Fat: 2.4g

Chapter no. 8 5&1 Meal Plan

In this chapter, there is a 28-day meal plan for you to follow and have a healthy diet if you have type 2 diabetes. It includes all the recipes that you can eat in your breakfast, A.M snack, Lunch, P.M snack and dinner.

8.1 Week 1

Day 1

Fueling recipes

- Lean and Green Biscuit Pizza
- Lean and Green Mint Thin Cookies
- Hummus with Pumpkin Roasted Beetroot Salad
- Yoghurt Icy Poles
- Lean and Green Watercress & Roasted Eggplant with Grilled Tempeh

Lean and Green recipes

- Chicken Crust Lean and Green Veggie Pizza

Day 2

Fueling recipes

- Lean and Green Peanut Butter Mini Cups
- Roasted Kale, Pumpkin, & Couscous Salad
- Yoghurt Icy Poles
- Lean and Green Orange Spiced Cranberry Cheesecake
- Hummus with Pumpkin Roasted Beetroot Salad

Lean and Green recipes

- Lean and Green Spinach Pizza & Chicken Alfredo

Day 3

Fueling recipes

- Tiramisu Milkshake Lean and Green
- Yoghurt Icy Poles
- Cooked Kumara Salad with Roasted Capsicum, Green Beans, & Mustard Seeds

- Lean and Green Cheesecake Mint Chocolate Muffins
- Hummus with Pumpkin Roasted Beetroot Salad

Lean and Green recipes

- Lean and Green Chicken Cauliflower Enchiladas

Day 4

Fueling recipes

- Caprese Lean and Green Pizza Bites
- Heirloom Feta and Mint with Tomato Salad
- Yoghurt Icy Poles
- Lean and Green Pinto's and Cheese
- Hummus with Pumpkin Roasted Beetroot Salad

Lean and Green recipes

- Lean and Green Shrimp Gumbo and Chicken

Day 5

Fueling recipes

- Fruit Popsicles
- Hummus with Pumpkin Roasted Beetroot Salad
- Hazelnuts with Green Salad
- Cheesy Spinach Lean and Green Smashed Potatoes
- Lean and Green Watercress & Roasted Eggplant with Grilled Tempeh

Lean and Green recipes

- Lean and Green Kohlrabi and Chicken Noodle Soup

Day 6

Fueling recipes

- Real Fruit Icy Poles

- Lean and Green Watercress & Roasted Eggplant with Grilled Tempeh
- Mushroom Bun Lean and Green Sliders
- Yoghurt Icy Poles
- Taco Stuffed Lean and Green Portabellos

Lean and Green recipes
- Lean and Green Chicken Potpie Cauliflower Crust

Day 7
Fueling recipes

- Lean and Green Buffalo and Chicken Meatballs
- Lean and Green Watercress & Roasted Eggplant with Grilled Tempeh
- Taco Stuffed Lean and Green Portabellos
- Coconut Colada Lean and Green
- Lean and Green Burgers Jalapeno Cheddar

Lean and Green recipes
Lean and Green Mediterranean Chicken Sheet Pan & Vegetables

8.2 Week 2
Day 1
Fueling recipes
- Neapolitan Froyo Lean and Green Popsicles
- Taco Stuffed Lean and Green Portabellos
- Lean and Green Beef Pot Stickers Cabbage Wrapped
- French Toast Lean and Green Sticks
- Easy and Healthy Salad Recipes

Lean and Green recipes
- Chicken Zoodle Lean and Green Alfredo

Day 2
Fueling recipes
- Lean and Green Peanut Butter Bites with Sugar
- Rainbow Salad
- Lean and Green Club Tacos
- Greek Yogurt Lean and Green Breakfast Bark
- Lean and Green Swai Fish Lemon Pepper with Parmesan Garlic Asparagus

Lean and Green recipes
- Pot Chicken Lean and Green Cacciatore

Day 3
Fueling recipes

- Lean and Green Pecan Muffins of Sweet Potato
- Tuna Nicoise Lean and Green Salad
- Lean and Green Burgers Jalapeno Cheddar
- Chocolate Milkshakes
- Mini Mac Lean and Green Salad

Lean and Green recipes
- Lean and Green Grilled Marinated Chicken Root Beer

Day 4
Fueling recipes
- Lean and Green Hemp & Coconut Green Smoothie
- Shrimp Campechana Lean and Green Salad
- Quest Chips Taco Lean and Green Salad
- Strawberry Smoothie
- Lean and Green Watercress & Roasted Eggplant with Grilled Tempeh

Lean and Green recipes
- Lean and Green Chicken Chili

Day 5
Fueling recipes
- Cucumber Cups
- Sheet Pan Lean and Green Lettuce Wraps, Chicken Fajita

122

- Lean and Green Greek Broiled Burger and Lettuce Wraps
- Hard Boil Eggs
- Salmon with Cucumber, Tomato, and Dill Salad

Lean and Green recipes

- Chicken and Paella with Soy Chorizo Lean and Green

Day 6

Fueling recipes

- Toast of Ricotta-Honey with Berries
- Lean and Green Zucchini and Turkey Meatballs Noodles
- Cumin Bistec Tacos Lean and Green

- Pistachio and Oat Bars
- Lamb Rack with Lentil Salad and Warm Apple

Lean and Green recipes

- Chicken Parmesan Lean and Green

Day 7

Fueling recipes

- Feta Dip
- Burgers with Herb-Feta Sauce
- Bibimbap Bowls Lean and Green
- Goat's Cheese and Pumpkin Salad
- Mac Salad Lean and Green

Lean and Green recipes

- Lean and Green Chicken Medley

8.3 Week 3

Day 1

Fueling recipes

- Lean and Green Biscuit Pizza
- Lean and Green Mint Thin Cookies
- Hummus with Pumpkin Roasted Beetroot Salad
- Yoghurt Icy Poles
- Lean and Green Watercress & Roasted Eggplant with Grilled Tempeh

Lean and Green recipes

- Chicken Crust Lean and Green Veggie Pizza

Day 2

Fueling recipes

- Lean and Green Peanut Butter Mini Cups
- Roasted Kale, Pumpkin, & Couscous Salad
- Yoghurt Icy Poles
- Lean and Green Orange Spiced Cranberry Cheesecake
- Hummus with Pumpkin Roasted Beetroot Salad

Lean and Green recipes

- Lean and Green Spinach Pizza & Chicken Alfredo

Day 3

Fueling recipes

- Tiramisu Milkshake Lean and Green
- Yoghurt Icy Poles
- Cooked Kumara Salad with Roasted Capsicum, Green Beans, & Mustard Seeds
- Lean and Green Cheesecake Mint Chocolate Muffins
- Hummus with Pumpkin Roasted Beetroot Salad

Lean and Green recipes

- Lean and Green Chicken Cauliflower Enchiladas

Day 4

Fueling recipes

- Caprese Lean and Green Pizza Bites
- Heirloom Feta and Mint with Tomato Salad
- Yoghurt Icy Poles
- Lean and Green Pinto's and Cheese
- Hummus with Pumpkin Roasted Beetroot Salad

Lean and Green recipes

- Lean and Green Shrimp Gumbo and Chicken

Day 5

Fueling recipes

- Fruit Popsicles
- Hummus with Pumpkin Roasted Beetroot Salad
- Hazelnuts with Green Salad
- Cheesy Spinach Lean and Green Smashed Potatoes
- Lean and Green Watercress & Roasted Eggplant with Grilled Tempeh

Lean and Green recipes
- Lean and Green Kohlrabi and Chicken Noodle Soup

Day 6
Fueling recipes
- Real Fruit Icy Poles
- Lean and Green Watercress & Roasted Eggplant with Grilled Tempeh
- Mushroom Bun Lean and Green Sliders
- Yoghurt Icy Poles

8.4 Week 4
Day 1
Fueling recipes
- Neapolitan Froyo Lean and Green Popsicles
- Taco Stuffed Lean and Green Portabellos
- Lean and Green Beef Pot Stickers Cabbage Wrapped
- French Toast Lean and Green Sticks
- Easy and Healthy Salad Recipes

Lean and Green recipes
- Chicken Zoodle Lean and Green Alfredo

Day 2
Fueling recipes
- Lean and Green Peanut Butter Bites with Sugar
- Rainbow Salad
- Lean and Green Club Tacos
- Greek Yogurt Lean and Green Breakfast Bark

- Taco Stuffed Lean and Green Portabellos

Lean and Green recipes
- Lean and Green Chicken Potpie Cauliflower Crust

Day 7
Fueling recipes
- Lean and Green Buffalo and Chicken Meatballs
- Lean and Green Watercress & Roasted Eggplant with Grilled Tempeh
- Taco Stuffed Lean and Green Portabellos
- Coconut Colada Lean and Green
- Lean and Green Burgers Jalapeno Cheddar

Lean and Green recipes
- Lean and Green Mediterranean Chicken Sheet Pan & Vegetables

- Lean and Green Swai Fish Lemon Pepper with Parmesan Garlic Asparagus

Lean and Green recipes
- Pot Chicken Lean and Green Cacciatore

Day 3
Fueling recipes
- Lean and Green Pecan Muffins of Sweet Potato
- Tuna Nicoise Lean and Green Salad
- Lean and Green Burgers Jalapeno Cheddar
- Chocolate Milkshakes
- Mini Mac Lean and Green Salad

Lean and Green recipes
- Lean and Green Grilled Marinated Chicken Root Beer

Day 4
Fueling recipes
- Lean and Green Hemp & Coconut Green Smoothie
- Shrimp Campechana Lean and Green Salad

- Quest Chips Taco Lean and Green Salad
- Strawberry Smoothie
- Lean and Green Watercress & Roasted Eggplant with Grilled Tempeh

Lean and Green recipes

- Lean and Green Chicken Chili

Day 5

Fueling recipes

- Cucumber Cups
- Sheet Pan Lean and Green Lettuce Wraps, Chicken Fajita
- Lean and Green Greek Broiled Burger and Lettuce Wraps
- Hard Boil Eggs
- Salmon with Cucumber, Tomato, and Dill Salad

Lean and Green recipes

- Chicken and Paella with Soy Chorizo Lean and Green

Day 6

Fueling recipes

- Toast of Ricotta-Honey with Berries
- Lean and Green Zucchini and Turkey Meatballs Noodles
- Cumin Bistec Tacos Lean and Green
- Pistachio and Oat Bars
- Lamb Rack with Lentil Salad and Warm Apple

Lean and Green recipes

- Chicken Parmesan Lean and Green

Day 7

Fueling recipes

- Feta Dip
- Burgers with Herb-Feta Sauce
- Bibimbap Bowls Lean and Green
- Goat's Cheese and Pumpkin Salad
- Mac Salad Lean and Green

Lean and Green recipes

- Lean and Green Chicken Medley

Conclusion

The FDA has given the weight-management program Optavia its approval. American Medical Association has taken this independent action (AMA). It's a diet regimen that has undergone rigorous scientific investigation and has been confirmed to be 100 percent effective. In order to improve weight loss, Optavia relies heavily on calorie restriction. Since most fuelings have 100 to 110 calories each, following this diet would allow you to consume around 1,000 Cals daily. Optavia diet works for normal people of every age and just demands that they adhere to this diet; no medical aid or monitoring is necessary. These are just a few of the amazing advantages Optavia has over certain other diet plans. In the first week of this program, someone may lose a maximum of three pounds, and they can keep losing weight steadily after that. If 3 pounds are not lost after a week, it is best to see a doctor. It has been discovered that the Optavia diet, which is low in fat and protein, may prevent obesity. Optavia diet doesn't call for significant way-of-life adjustments.

Optavia diet has a set of three regimens, two of which focus on losing weight and improving weight management. Foods on a diet are more protein-rich and fewer in calories and carbohydrates to encourage weight loss. Each method requires you to eat half of the meals in pre-packaged Optavia food. It is a relatively good diet for nutritious eating because the menu suggests consuming carbohydrates and protein but healthy fat. Experts concur that Optavia may help with weight loss due to its diet's favorable calorie intake. It's unlikely to drastically alter the eating habits, however. Once you stop your diet, you'll probably gain the weight back. Thus, the Optavia diet has shown to be quite effective in regulating weight maintenance. Through reduced calories, prepackaged foods, homemade cuisine with simple carbs, and individualized coaching, the Optavia Weight Reduction Plan encourages weight loss. The Optavia diet promotes weight loss via the use of low-calorie prepared meals, naturally low-carb dinners, and specialized instruction. Unfortunately, the diet is expensive, monotonous, and doesn't satisfy every dietary need. Additionally, increased calorie restriction may result in a lack of supplements and other serious health issues. In addition, because this strategy stimulates rapid weight & fat reduction, further study is required to determine if it also fosters the long-term behavioral changes required for success. In conclusion, I hope you learned that Optavia Diet is primarily intended to aid individuals in losing weight and is intended to be taken for a brief period of time.